D0641686

A GUIDE
TO THE
TEXAS
MEDICAL
CENTER

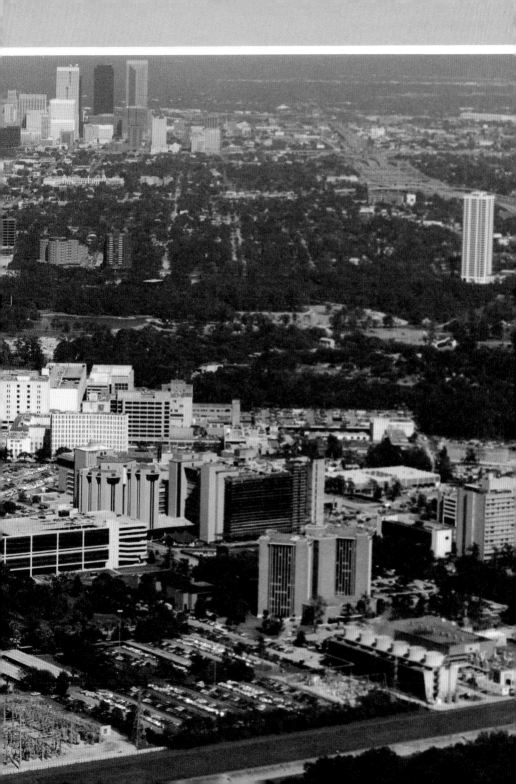

A GUIDE
TO THE

TEXAS
MEDICAL
CENTER

BY
CLYDE W. BURLESON
AND
SUZY WILLIAMS BURLESON

UNIVERSITY OF TEXAS PRESS
AUSTIN

Special thanks to Mary Schiflett, Joe Sigler, and members of Texas Medical Center's Public Relations Advisory Council. We also wish to acknowledge the historical research of Anne Sieber.

First Edition, 1987

Library of Congress Cataloging-in-Publication Data

Burleson, Clyde W., 1934–
    A guide to the Texas Medical Center.

    Includes index.
    1. Texas Medical Center—Description—Guide-books.
2. Texas Medical Center—Directories. 3. Medical
centers—Texas—Houston—Description—Guide-books.
4. Medical centers—Texas—Houston—Directories.
I. Burleson, Suzy Williams. II. Title.
RA982.H62T493   1987   362.1'1'097641411   86-16152
ISBN 0-292-72727-5 (pbk.)

CONTENTS

LIST OF MAPS

The Texas Medical Center is more than buildings of brick and concrete; more than nuclear reactors and X-ray machines; more, even, than the sum of all those who have given so much, all those who have come before.

The Texas Medical Center is a place in time. It exists because some individuals dared to plan and dream, others to contribute their fortunes, and still more to devote every waking hour to a pursuit of excellence in diagnosis, treatment, teaching, communications, and research.

How it came to be, and what it is today, would be difficult to encompass in a single volume, but that is not the purpose of this book. This guide to the Medical Center is designed to serve the over two million persons who annually come here for help, learning, work, visitation, and the myriad other reasons people find each day to "go to the center."

For the first-time visitor, this book will provide directions and instructions on parking. For the "regular," there is information on facilities other than those visited in a normal routine. For anyone who is interested, there is background on every component and institution, phone numbers, and an overview of the Medical Center not available elsewhere.

It is hoped that patients, visitors, volunteers, workers, medical staffs, administrative personnel, visiting scientists, sales people, delivery drivers, and all who come to the Medical Center will find this book useful. It was written to serve a number of needs and points of view, which, in turn, ensures some shortcomings. It is difficult to encompass so many divergent interests and still discuss deeply each distinct installation. Consistency, then, has been the rule. Each organization, school, hospital, or facility has been treated as equally as possible.

This book should help to eliminate some of the mystery and trepidation felt by infrequent visitors, while giving frequenters new insights and information that will be useful in their daily routines.

All the statistics and figures quoted for the Texas Medical Center and its member institutions are based on the latest data available when this book went to press. Changes occur frequently and specific questions should be directed to the individual facilities.

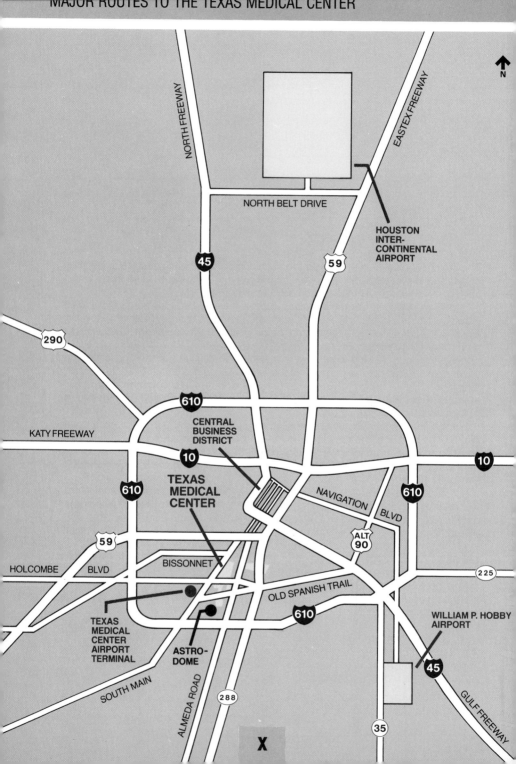

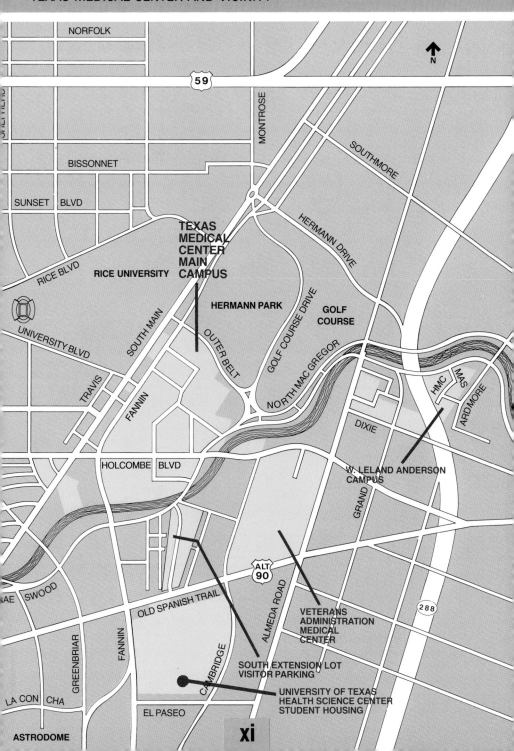

N

NORFOLK

59

MONTROSE

SOUTHMORE

BISSONNET

HERMANN DRIVE

SUNSET BLVD

RICE BLVD

RICE UNIVERSITY

TEXAS MEDICAL CENTER MAIN CAMPUS

HERMANN PARK

GOLF COURSE

SOUTH MAIN

OUTER BELT

GOLF COURSE DRIVE

NORTH MAC GREGOR

UNIVERSITY BLVD

TRAVIS

FANNIN

HMC

MAS

ARDMORE

DIXIE

HOLCOMBE BLVD

W. LELAND ANDERSON CAMPUS

GRAND

SWOOD

ALT 90

OLD SPANISH TRAIL

VETERANS ADMINISTRATION MEDICAL CENTER

288

GREENBRIAR

FANNIN

CAMBRIDGE

ALMEDA ROAD

SOUTH EXTENSION LOT VISITOR PARKING

LA CON CHA

EL PASEO

UNIVERSITY OF TEXAS HEALTH SCIENCE CENTER STUDENT HOUSING

ASTRODOME

xi

TEXAS MEDICAL CENTER
MAIN CAMPUS

RICE UNIVERSITY

HERMANN PARK

N

OUTER BELT DRIVE

SOUTH MAIN

FANNIN

HERMANN GARAGE

1

3A

3B

3C

2

4

ROSS STERLING

G4

BEN TAUB GARAGE

9

G3

8

7

M.D. ANDERSON

5

6A

10E

10B

BELLOWS POLICE

11A

E. CULLEN

10D

11C

11B

10C

11D

6B

6C

10A

12

6D

WILKINS

MOURSUND

G1

G6

13

LAMAR FLEMING

23

FANNIN

14

18

15

22

20

19C

19D

16

BERTNER

21

19A

17

19B

JOHN FREEMAN

BATES

G2

BATES

25

G5

MAC GREGOR

TO W. LELAND ANDERSON CAMPUS

HOLCOMBE

24

RICHARD J.V. JOHNSON AVE

26

19E

27

HERMAN PRESSLER

STAFFORDSHIRE

CAMBRIDGE

SOUTH EXTENSION LOT
VISITOR PARKING

BRAYS BAYOU

WYNDALE

BRAESWOOD

xii

28

TEXAS MEDICAL CENTER
W. LELAND ANDERSON CAMPUS

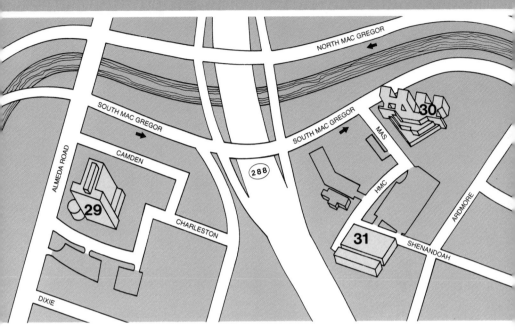

HISTORY

The Texas Medical Center has two histories. One is medical, focusing on doctors' and scientists' achievements in health care and research. The other deals with founders, fund raisers, and finance. Both are important. One would not endure without the other; and the Medical Center would not exist if either had not happened.

A most unusual fact about the Texas Medical Center is that it was not originally conceived by doctors. Businessmen generated the idea, sold it to the community, and guided the early planning.

To understand the Medical Center, it is necessary to understand the Houston that was—Houston of the thirties, forties, and fifties. It was a city like no other, ever—a place just beginning to feel its potential, to savor its growing strength. People, bold enough to dream, brave enough to act, had already altered America's face to the commercial world by dredging the Houston Ship Channel and making the city a major port. Others, of equal vision, had cut their marks in cotton, timber, oil, banking, rail, and trade. As fortunes grew, so too did a sense of obligation to the town that had given these millionaires a place to work and to show their wares. Much of the story of Houston's growth is traceable to these great philanthropists—men and women who, when confronted by a need, gave of their time and money to seek a solution, asking in return only that Houston be bigger and better.

The spirit of the city's financial leaders through three decades formed a foundation for the explosive growth of the sixties, seventies, and eighties. The Texas Medical Center is a product of this era of progressive, daring, and clear thinking, when anything was possible and the hardest task was to conceive of yet another way to bring Houston into national and international prominence.

Intelligence, money, enthusiasm, and a willingness to venture all on a single idea beget more of the same. People who possess these qualities attract individuals of like character. So it is little wonder that those who came to the Medical Center as leaders, to train, treat, and perform research, soon earned respect for themselves, their staffs, and the institutions they guided.

There, in brief, is the real history of the Texas Medical Center. It was conceived by dynamic people in an era and place where challenge was greeted as opportunity. It was staffed by individuals who placed creative competence in their professions above all else. Any outcome other than growth was inconceivable. And, because growth alone was insufficient, both philanthropists and scientists devoted their attention to a common goal of excellence—excellence in facilities, excellence in health care, excellence in teaching, and excellence in research.

The Texas Medical Center is a product of a variety of individuals—so many who made meaningful contributions that it would take volumes to tell of them all. A few, however, can be singled out—not to recite their life stories but to place them in context with the creation, development, and growth of one of the most successful of Houston's grand projects, the Texas Medical Center.

Hermann Hospital is the oldest building on the site. Built fifteen years before the rest of the Medical Center was initiated, it is named after its eccentrically frugal benefactor, George Hermann. Born of poor Swiss immigrants in 1843, he had no close relatives after his second brother died in 1872. Hermann never married. A typical Hermann story holds that once, when out riding one morning with two friends, he refused to go into a restaurant with them. He preferred to wait outside on the stoop and eat peanuts instead of paying for a restaurant meal. His doctor tells how Hermann gave up eggs for breakfast when he found out they cost sixty cents a dozen. "Until eggs get cheaper," Hermann said, "prunes are good enough." Although he owned several estates, they were all rented out. Hermann chose to live in a single room amid one of his tenant families.

He learned frugality from his parents, who had arrived in America with five dollars. When it came to being a patron, Hermann's sympathies lay not with education or the arts but with the poor. He donated 278 acres to the city. This site, immediately north of the Medical Center, is today called Hermann Park. It is a center of Houston weekend recreation, as well as serving as a pleasant mixer of the predominantly white university neighborhoods with the predominantly black neighborhoods to the east. He also bequeathed Hermann Square in front of the city hall, downtown. Hermann said he intended it as a "breathing space" for all Houstonians. In order to make it so, he obtained a special city ordinance permitting overnight sleeping. Because Hermann owned a lumber company, stories have it that he had this square in mind to provide a haven for his lumberjacks when they passed out during their weekend drunks in the city.

Dominating this unusual man's contributions to Houston is Hermann Hospital, which opened in 1925, nine years after his death.

George Hermann was responsible for the first hospital in what was to become the Texas Medical Center. But the man to whom the Medical Center owes its existence is Monroe D. Anderson.

Anderson came to Houston in 1907 as a representative of the largest cotton trading firm in the world, Anderson, Clayton & Company, of which he later became president. Few remember much about Anderson; he was a modest man with a strong American work ethic.

Like Hermann, Anderson never married, and at the age of 63, in 1936, he founded the M. D. Anderson Foundation with an endowment of $300,000. Anderson named himself and two of his lawyers, John Henry Freeman and Colonel William B. Bates, trustees; the three had become friends as fishing companions, and it was on their angling expeditions that they worked out the goals of their new foundation. (Freeman and Bates were partners in the law firm of Fulbright, Crooker, Freeman, & Bates, which exists today as Fulbright & Jaworski.) The foundation's first gift was a check of $1,000 to the Junior League Eye Fund for eyeglasses. A little over two years after establishing M. D. Anderson Foundation, Anderson died, leaving $19 million to the organization.

The public never recognized Anderson as a philanthropist during his lifetime. Neither of Houston's two major newspapers even mentioned the existence of the M. D. Anderson Foundation in his obituary, although both found it important enough to note that he was an Elk. No one had any idea that Anderson was going to bequeath all his investments to his foundation, and when he died the trustees (led by Horace Wilkins, who succeeded Anderson) were left with an enormous amount of money. Up to that time, it was the largest available charitable fund ever created in Texas. Yet scarcely any directions for its use existed. The trustees tried to develop a project in keeping with Anderson's philosophy. At first, they had no special concept in mind. Then, little by little, an innovative, original idea began to take hold. Hospitals of the time were basically designed to serve the wealthy or the very needy. The trustees talked of a facility for the average person, the individual who would be financially ruined if serious illness struck. They reached agreement and took fast action.

In 1941, the state legislature voted to grant the University of Texas $500,000 for the purpose of starting a cancer research hospital. The M. D. Anderson Foundation then took its first major action by proposing to match the state's gift and to supply the necessary land, provided the hospital was located in Houston. In August 1942, the offer was accepted and the projected institution was called M. D. Anderson Hospital for Cancer Research. The next problem was to find a site. Houston businessmen rallied to the cause and solved this problem through a special election concerning the sale of 134 acres of wooded property a couple of miles southwest of the city to the Anderson Foundation. The proposal passed (with only 741 votes cast), and the city sold the land in December of 1943 for $100,000.

In addition to finding a location, the Medical Center also found its second and third institutions. In that same year, 1943, Baylor University College of Medicine was having difficulties with its home in Dallas. The M. D. Anderson Foundation offered $1 million for construction of a facility and $100,000 a year for the next ten years if Baylor would come to Houston. The Houston Chamber of Commerce added $500,000 to the bid, and Baylor accepted. Also in 1943, the Texas Dental College under Frederick C. Elliot, D.D.S., became the University of Texas School of Dentistry and joined the group.

The idea for the center was congealing. In 1945, it incorporated as Texas Medical Center and was presented with the deed to the 134 acres by the M. D. Anderson Foundation. The public was beginning to take notice of the massive project that was being initiated way down in the forested area next to Rice University; by 1946, newspapers were filled with headlines about the "New $100,000,000 Medical Center." However, despite the formalization of the plan, there were to be no buildings on the new site for another four years (besides the already existing Hermann Hospital); all three of the fledgling institutions were to be housed in temporary quarters. In 1943 when Baylor made the transfer from Dallas to its temporary location, the old Sears & Roebuck building, it had to move in the short time between the end of classes in May and the beginning of a new semester in July. The dental college stayed at its old location at Fannin and Blodgett, and M. D. Anderson moved into the old Baker estate, The Oaks, in 1944.

Dr. E. William Bertner, a Houston physician for twenty-nine years, was a close friend of several Anderson Foundation trustees. He lived on the same floor of the Rice Hotel as John Freeman. Dr. Bertner contributed a valuable medical perspective to the Medical Center development sessions and served as acting director of M. D. Anderson from 1942 to 1946.

In 1946, Dr. R. Lee Clark became M. D. Anderson's first permanent director. Dr. Clark held this post until 1968, when he was named the hospital's first president. As the cancer research institution was at a disadvantage because of its newness and its as yet limited supply of funds, Clark decided that research efforts would be more fruitful if they focused on a few specific areas instead of trying to cover the entire field of cancer study. To begin, biochemists concentrated on carbohydrate metabolism and protein metabolism at the cellular level. Biologists worked toward isolating the genetic origin of cancer, and physicists tried to pinpoint the effects on the body of cobalt gamma rays, betatron X rays, and normal X rays. The hospital's first accomplishment was publication of the *Manual of the M. D. Anderson Hospital for Cancer Research,* which tried to explain "the more recent methods in diagnosis and treatment of cancer." In 1946, the hospital held its first in a series of annual symposia on cancer. These still continue today. M. D. Anderson's physics department was started by Dr. Leonard Grimmett, who had a leading role in designing the important Cobalt-60 irradiator. The research center obtained an early model of one of these mega-instruments in 1953.

In 1947, the first new structure on the Medical Center's vast land was ready for occupancy—Baylor's Cullen Building. Also, after having expanded in 1938 and 1944, Hermann Hospital added its splendid new 375-bed Robertson Pavilion in 1949. In the same year the fourteen-story Hermann Professional Building was erected on Main Street. In 1951, Methodist Hospital moved into its new quarters with the distinctive and gigantic tile mural façade depicting Christ on the cross flanked by medical scenarios. The Houston Speech and Hearing Institute joined the Medical Center at the same time. The following year Methodist formed an alliance with Baylor, serving as a teaching hospital for the university while benefiting from the additional help and expertise. Also established in 1952 was the Arabia Temple Crippled Children's Clinic (later called the Shriners Hospital for Crippled Children). In 1954, another religiously affiliated group joined the Medical Center— St. Luke's Episcopal Hospital. Texas Children's Hospital was subsequently built that year and joined to St. Luke's. Texas Children's was largely funded by the Pin Oaks Horse Show, a special event sponsored initially by the Abercrombie family and looked forward to annually in Houston. With the erection of the Jesse H. Jones Library Building in 1954, the Texas Medical Center could already boast of eleven institutions: four hospitals, two children's hospitals, a university, a library, a speech and hearing center, a dental school, and an overall planning and coordinating group.

In 1948, one year after Baylor moved into its permanent residence, the university staff made what proved to be an equally important acquisition: Dr. Michael Ellis DeBakey, a young, ambitious assistant professor from Louisiana, was brought to head the surgery department.

Houstonians were already proud of their Medical Center for its big buildings, its expensive equipment, and its dependable patient care; Michael DeBakey made Houston aware of its magnificent research and treatment. Breaking with long-standing medical tradition of reserve and nonpublicity, DeBakey courted the media to tell his story, alienating many local physicians. DeBakey televised a heart operation on "March for Medicine," in October of 1954. The medical community was surprised and outraged. DeBakey confidently maintained that the public ought to know what it was paying for. No one could deny that the publicity was helping Baylor and Methodist Hospital, where DeBakey was doing his operating. Important people were flying in from all over the world for Dr. DeBakey's famous heart surgery.

His specialty was repair and replacement of weakened blood vessels with grafts. He perfected the procedure of bypassing the aneurysm with either a grafted piece of blood vessel taken from the leg or a Dacron graft, even applying the Dacron graft directly to the weakened area.

Two recent innovations had opened up the field of heart surgery: the catheter and the heart-lung oxygenating machine, the "pump." The catheter is a slender tube that can be inserted into an exterior vein and then snaked into the heart as a probe. The pump is used as a heart and lung bypass: blood flows into the pump, is oxygenated, and then is pulsed back into the body, leaving the heart free to be cut open. Before the pump, open-heart surgery was not possible.

DeBakey, however, was not initially involved in open-heart techniques; it took a younger protégé to make Houston one of the centers of heart surgery—Denton Cooley. Cooley came to Baylor in 1951. Heart operations using "pumps" were his specialty, and he soon came to do more of them and to do them faster than any other person. The key to both DeBakey's and Cooley's success was their endurance and rapidity in operating, for speed is of the essence in heart surgery; Cooley got so he could do a "pump" in a mind-boggling twenty-eight minutes. Whereas many heart surgeons only did one operation a day, DeBakey and Cooley regularly did six to ten. Both men were driven with a superhuman energy that seemed unrelenting. Once Cooley operated a full day in pain from a hernia; after finishing his last case he lay down on the operating table himself and let his assistant do a surgical repair.

The tension caused by Cooley and DeBakey's intensity finally snapped—against each other. Cooley moved his operations to St. Luke's, severing all relations with

DeBakey. Soon after Cooley left, DeBakey started doing open-heart operations. In 1962, Cooley opened the seven-story Texas Heart Institute in St. Luke's. It was here he performed several controversial heart transplants.

Meanwhile, the Medical Center continued to expand. The Institute for Rehabilitation and Research was opened in 1959. At TIRR, intensive rehabilitation was available for those handicapped by injury, illness, or birth defect. In 1960, the Texas Research Institute of Mental Sciences was opened. The Institute of Religion, chartered in 1955, moved from temporary quarters in the library building to its present four-story structure that year. In 1960, Texas Woman's University established its Houston campus, offering degree programs in most of the health care professions. In 1963, the much needed charity hospital, Ben Taub, was erected. In 1965, the Houston Health Department joined the other members of the Medical Center, as did Prairie View A&M University College of Nursing in 1968. In 1976, the Life Flight helicopter rescue program started flying as a service of Hermann Hospital. Operating within a 150-mile radius, the Life Flight helicopter primarily handles trauma victims, although it also transports cardiac patients, others with serious medical problems, and critically ill newborns.

The Medical Center's momentous growth has paralleled Houston's. Far from being on the outskirts of the city as it was originally, it is now considered centrally located. It has twelve hospitals or patient care facilities, nine academic institutions, and many specialized support and public service facilities. Far from the envisioned "$100 million medical complex," total capital investment has recently exceeded $1.5 billion, with over a quarter of that amount coming from private gifts. Its annual operating costs are in excess of $1.5 billion. The Medical Center expanded yet more with the addition of St. Anthony Center, Veterans Administration Medical Center, and a 1985 acquisition of 22.6 acres adjacent to the main campus. It has grown from its original 137 acres on the edge of Hermann Park to more than 525 acres.

Glamorous Houston names have been integrally associated with the Texas Medical Center: Hermann, Cullen, Jesse Jones, Ben Taub, Hobby, Jaworski, Scurlock, Weingarten, and many others. Houstonians have infused their own peculiar vitality into the Medical Center. In a few short decades it has grown into one of the world's finest medical complexes. The fusing together of three different worlds—those of the businessperson, the healer, and the scientist—has produced one of the most remarkable achievements in medical history.

Jesse H. Jones Library Building
1133 M. D. Anderson Blvd. (77030)
713/797-0100

HOURS
M−F, 8 AM−5 PM
PARKING
Garage #3; Garage #4; short-term meters in
front of building (quarters only)
RECEPTION
Fourth floor

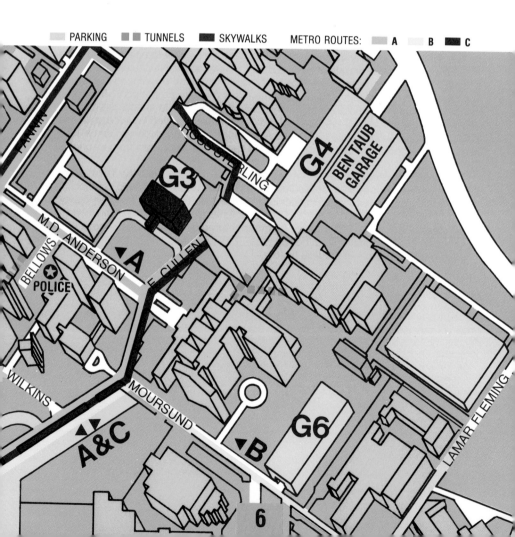

Texas Medical Center is the planning and coordinating body for the 525 acres in the South Main area. It provides and maintains cooperative programs and services, and is a catalyst for ideas, the planner of projects that serve mutual interests for all Medical Center institutions. Members of the board of directors are drawn from the legal and business professions of the Houston community.

Among the cooperative programs it supports is the Assistance Center (790-1136), also known as the Visitor Information Center (see p. 8).

The Office of Public Affairs publishes *Texas Medical Center News* (668-0567), a free monthly periodical for employees, students, patients, and visitors. The newspaper focuses on news and activities at the Medical Center. Copies may be found in all institutions and at various places throughout the area.

The Renilda Hilkemeyer Child Care Center (747-2173), located at 5614 H.M.C. Street, is a preschool, child care facility for children of Medical Center workers who find it difficult to use other nurseries because of unusual working hours. It is open from 6:00 AM to midnight. Children six to twelve years old receive night, weekend, and holiday care. Fees are subsidized by many institutions as an employee benefit.

The Police Department (795-0000), at 1120 M. D. Anderson Boulevard, is a certified police agency employing and training a force of officers who have full powers of arrest (see p. 111).

The residence hall program includes a centrally located high-rise building, where students and nursing personnel can rent furnished, reasonably priced apartments in Laurence H. Favrot Hall (6540 Bellows Lane, 797-0962). Favrot Hall has 155 apartments, each with a kitchenette.

The Parking Department (1522 Braeswood, north entrance to the remote South Extension Lot, 797-9445) has responsibility for the multideck parking garages and off-campus park-and-ride facilities. It coordinates transportation around the complex and contracts with METRO for shuttle service throughout the complex (see p. 116).

The Computer Service Center bears responsibility for data collection and analysis of the Texas Medical Center operations.

The Maintenance Department maintains streets, walks, entrances, parking lots, garages, certain buildings, and common grounds; it also coordinates architectural and site-planning responsibilities. A groundskeeping service is provided for contracting institutions.

Other cooperative services were developed by Texas Medical Center and have now become separate member institutions with independent leadership. Texas Medical Center Central Heating and Cooling Services Cooperative Association is a huge heating and cooling plant, which furnishes chilled and hot water to many institutions at discount rates. Texas Medical Center Hospital Laundry Cooperative Association is a specialized laundry facility used by nonprofit member institutions inside and outside the Medical Center.

ASSISTANCE CENTER

Garage #2
1155 Holcombe Blvd. (77030)
713/790-1136

HOURS
M–F, 9 AM–5 PM

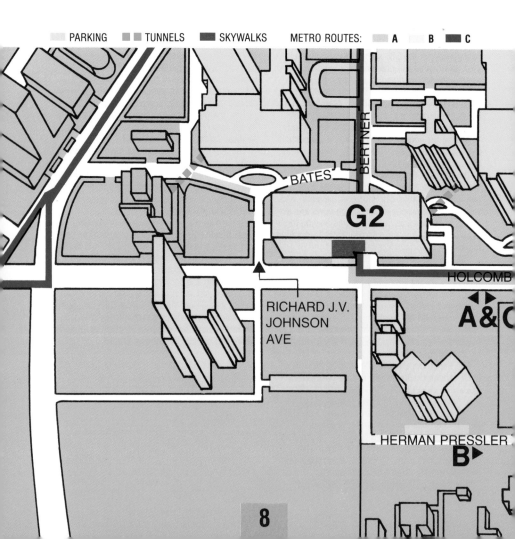

PARKING   TUNNELS   SKYWALKS   METRO ROUTES: A   B   C

BERTNER

BATES

G2

HOLCOMB

RICHARD J.V. JOHNSON AVE

A&C

HERMAN PRESSLER

B▶

Working from Garage #2 (ground level, corner of Holcombe Blvd. and Bertner Ave.), the Assistance Center is one of the most vital resources for patients and individuals with an interest in the Texas Medical Center.

Staffed by professionals and members of the Assistance League of Houston, who maintain an information desk, this one-stop facility can provide details on short- and long-term housing, restaurants, entertainment, recreational activities, shopping centers, and available services. It can also refer individuals to specific patient relations units in the various hospitals.

One of the key offerings of the Assistance Center is its guided tours. The tours last approximately a half hour, are free, and are available Monday through Friday at 10:00 AM or by special arrangement. Films and videotapes explaining the Medical Center can be shown prior to leaving. For groups, such as a class of students, a medical association, or any large number of people, advance arrangements need to be made with the tour coordinator.

The Assistance Center also has a full display of hospital brochures and a number of general information folders.

Free van service to the museum area, Houston Zoo, and University Village shopping area is offered for employees, visitors, and patients' families on certain weekdays. Call the Assistance Center for specific information.

Able Express, a shop that carries a variety of aids for disabled people, is quartered in a room at the Assistance Center. The store stocks kitchen utensils, dishes, housework aids, special tools, remote switches, and fascinating gadgets to make everyday life easier for the disabled. A list of items is available at the store. A project of the Assistance League, the shop is open Monday through Friday, 10:00 AM to 2:00 PM. Items are sold at cost.

BAYLOR COLLEGE OF MEDICINE

One Baylor Plaza (77030)
713/799-4951
Security: 799-4809

HOURS
M–F, 8 AM–5 PM
PARKING
Garage #6; Garage #4
RECEPTION
Cullen Bldg. off Alkek Fountain; Jones /
Anderson entrance

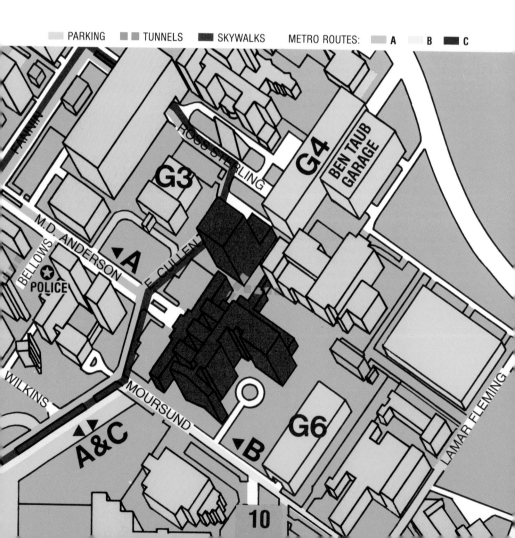

PARKING   TUNNELS   SKYWALKS   METRO ROUTES: A   B   C

The college was founded in 1900 as the Medical Department of the University of Dallas. Three years later, it became associated with Baylor University of Waco and, in 1943, moved to Houston from Dallas.

Baylor became the first educational institution of the Texas Medical Center in 1947, when it shifted from temporary facilities into the Cullen Building.

In 1969, Baylor University College of Medicine separated from Baylor University and became an independent institution. Since then it has been known as Baylor College of Medicine. It is the only private medical school in the Greater Southwest.

Baylor is dedicated to the promotion of health and the triumph over disease through education, research, and service. It was originally established to educate physicians, but medical training has since been expanded to include studies for researchers and allied health personnel.

Baylor's program is designed to give students a strong foundation in basic medical and clinical sciences. The school has received the maximum accreditation that can be given. In 1981 the Liaison Committee on Medical Education certified the college for a decade.

The usual medical course at Baylor takes four years, but a flexible curriculum allows students also to pursue research and graduate studies. Baylor is one of the few schools in the United States with a combined M.D./Ph.D. program for students interested in research careers.

The Graduate School offers advanced degrees in basic sciences, audiology, speech pathology, experimental biology, neuroscience, biochemical virology, cardiovascular sciences, psychology, and radiology. Graduate education is also available in clinical sciences in the largest such program in Texas. Baylor offers subspecialties in plastic, orthopedic, and thoracic surgery.

Baylor's residency program is the largest in the state. Over half its graduates enter primary care fields. Residency training ranges from three to seven years, depending on the specialty. Additionally, many young physicians take further fellowship schooling in subspecialties, such as pediatric cardiology.

Students and residents receive much of their experience in eight affiliated teaching hospitals in the Medical Center and the general Houston area. Baylor physicians are on staff at these facilities and many serve as chiefs-of-service at Texas Children's Hospital and Methodist Hospital. Other primary affiliated institutions include Ben Taub General Hospital, Jefferson Davis Hospital, Quentin R. Mease Community Hospital, Veterans Administration Medical Center, Institute for Rehabilitation and Research, and St. Luke's Episcopal Hospital. Baylor is also affiliated with other units in the Medical Center, Houston, and the state. Students have even had the opportunity to study tropical medicine courses at the Universidad Peruana Cayetano Heredia in Lima, Peru.

The college emphasizes the education of allied health personnel through its Center for Allied Health Professions. It offers certificate courses in allied health administration and teacher education, cardiac rehabilitation, nuclear medicine, and radiation therapy technology. The center has a physician's assistant program that leads to a bachelor of science degree.

Baylor was instrumental in forming the High School for Health Professions in 1972 with the Houston Independent School District. Its Center for Allied Health Professions cooperates with HISD in directing and operating this magnet school, which exposes high schoolers to the health care field and prepares them to continue academic and professional training.

Instruction at Baylor is not limited to students and residents. Beginning in 1974, many continuing education courses for physicians and other professionals have offered the latest information in patient care and research. One of the most comprehensive such programs in the United States, it has attracted some thirty thousand registrants in recent years.

Baylor has become known worldwide as a leader in basic and clinical research on a variety of illnesses and conditions. Scientists are constantly developing new methods of diagnosis and investigating new treatments for disease.

Baylor has the only Influenza Research Center in the nation, where work continues on the prevention, spread, and treatment of flu. The center has developed a new flu therapy using ribavarin (an antiviral drug) in aerosol form.

The Children's Nutrition Research Center seeks understanding of nutrition and its function in children's growth to healthy adulthood. Studies have focused on the effects of malnutrition in development and on the benefits of human breast milk compared to formula.

The unique DeBakey Heart Center carries on basic and clinical research into the cause, prevention, diagnosis, and treatment of conditions that affect the cardiovascular system.

Glaucoma patients receive the latest diagnosis and treatment at the Glaucoma Service and Research Laboratory. This lab, which serves as a prototype for similar labs being established in other parts of the country, tests and evaluates patients under a large number of criteria. Self-care of glaucoma is an important objective of the center.

Baylor's Cystic Fibrosis Center offers prenatal carrier testing and diagnosis for the affliction considered to be one of the most common life-threatening genetic diseases.

Research being conducted at the Sleep Disorders Center investigates nighttime respiration, sleep paralysis, insomnia, hypersomnia, sleep walking and talking, muscle spasms, and bed-wetting, among other problems.

Baylor's Pain Control and Biofeedback Clinic has been searching for new devices and psychological techniques for treating chronic pain.

Baylor's recently established Center for Biotechnology will work on developing new technologies to prevent, diagnose, and treat cancer, acquired immune deficiency syndrome (AIDS), and neurological disorders, among others.

Researchers and physicians are studying a wide range of other topics, such as cell function in cancer, fertility, allergy and immunological disorders, epilepsy, stroke, neuromuscular disease, spinal cord injury and rehabilitation engineering, Parkinson's disease, human genetics, birth defects, diabetes and endocrinology, and stuttering. Motion sickness studies have led to help for space sickness in astronauts. New immunodiagnostic methods are being devised to use monoclonal antibodies for cancer diagnosis.

The college continues its growth in many areas of learning and investigation. Along with that, Baylor has had to meet demands for physical expansion. Construction was completed in 1986 on the new East Campus, which includes a nine-story research tower, animal research facilities, and a supporting power plant.

Baylor has an operational biomedical magnetic resonance imaging (MRI) center at the 150-acre research complex at The Woodlands. MRI is a research and diagnostic device that allows physicians to visualize what is happening inside the human body without using radiation or invasive materials. Baylor was the first institution in Texas to use an MRI system, and it has two units in use at the Medical Center.

BCM Technologies, Inc., a subsidiary of Baylor, was created in 1984 to assist the transfer of recent medical technology to the consumer market.

One of Baylor's most outstanding assets is Michael E. DeBakey, M.D., chancellor of the college. Widely recognized as a surgeon, innovator, teacher, and medical statesman, he has worked tirelessly for the development of the college. His contributions have played a significant part in the growth and worldwide recognition of the institution.

In one of many landmark actions, Dr. DeBakey and a group of associates performed the first successful heart bypass operation in 1964. This procedure was made possible by a pump he had devised as a medical student. The open-heart operation has helped uncounted thousands of patients since that time. He has also developed more than fifty surgical instruments.

In February 1984, Dr. DeBakey performed his first heart transplant at Methodist Hospital since 1970. He predicted that the new transplant facility (located in the Fondren-Brown Building) at Methodist Hospital would be able to offer heart, lung, liver, bone marrow, and even pancreatic tissue transplants, along with kidney transplants, using the antirejection drug cyclosporine.

Author of more than one thousand books and articles, this prominent educator has received the Medal of Freedom, which is the highest award the president of the United States can bestow on a civilian. His devotion to the growth and excellence of Baylor College of Medicine will have a continuing forceful impact on the school for many years to come.

FOOD SERVICE
A cafeteria in the basement is open for breakfast and lunch, 6:45 AM to 10:00 AM and 11:30 AM to 2:00 PM. A faculty dining room is adjacent to the cafeteria in the Cullen Building.

SHOPPING FACILITIES
A bookstore located in the basement of the Cullen Building is open from 8:30 AM to 4:30 PM. It has medical texts, office supplies, greeting cards, magazines, paperbacks, candy, gum, and limited gift items.

LIBRARY FACILITIES
Baylor's Department of Otorhinolaryngology has one of the two Medical Center libraries (the other is the UT Neuroscience Library) under contract to the Houston Academy of Medicine–TMC Library for the provision of library services. A professional librarian is available for reference, computer data base searches, cataloging, book and journal acquisitions, and management. The Otorhinolaryngology Library provides immediate on-site access to core materials for faculty, residents, and staff in this specialized field. A learning resource center is on the second floor of the DeBakey Building. Students have access to video and audio tapes to review or to familiarize themselves with procedures.

GUIDED TOURS
Tours of the DeBakey Center teaching facilities are offered from September through May. Call 799-4712 to make arrangements. A medical museum in the DeBakey Center basement was recently opened.

GENERAL INFORMATION
Baylor maintains a Physicians Referral Service (799-6119), which can help patients find physicians in the Texas Medical Center in specific specialties. Requests for admission to the College may be made by phone (799-4841) or by writing to the Office of Admissions.

Baylor has two publications, *Baylor Medicine* and *Inside Information,* each published eleven times a year for faculty, staff, students, alumni, and friends.

The corten steel sculpture by Mark di Suvero in front of the Michael E. DeBakey Center is titled *Pranath Yama,* a Hindu phrase that deals with the cycle of life and death. Another work of art worthy of note is the untitled fresco by David Novros located in the DeBakey Building.

1502 Taub Loop (77030)
713/791-7000
Security: 791-7002

HOURS
Clinic: M–F, 8 AM–2 PM
Visiting: M–Sa, 1 PM–2 PM, 6:30 PM–8 PM;
Su & holidays, 1 PM–3 PM, 6:30 PM–8 PM
Emergency: 24 hours daily (791-7300)
PARKING
Ben Taub Parking Garage
RECEPTION
Lobby of hospital; outpatient clinic

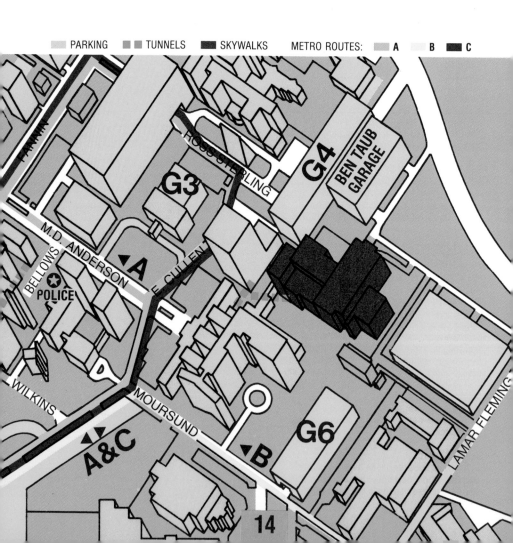

PARKING   TUNNELS   SKYWALKS   METRO ROUTES: A   B   C

Ben Taub is the general hospital of the Harris County Hospital District (HCHD). It is a tax-supported acute general health care and treatment facility, providing for financially indigent residents of Houston and of Harris County. All medical specialties are offered to those in need, except obstetrics, which is currently handled at Jefferson Davis, HCHD'S other hospital.

Built in the Texas Medical Center in 1963, it is a teaching facility for Baylor College of Medicine, which staffs the institution with physicians, residents, interns, medical students, and pupils in allied health programs.

Because the needy population is increasing, employees and staff of Ben Taub face and meet a daily challenge, fulfilling legal and humanitarian obligations. Limited resources and available space have made it necessary to create new methods and techniques of providing the finest medical care.

Houston has an urgent demand for public medical facilities, and plans for expansion are already underway. A proposed 550-bed Greater Ben Taub Hospital, a replacement hospital to be built in the place of the old parking garage, is intended for completion in early 1989.

At present, Ben Taub makes use of an auxiliary unit located three miles east of the Medical Center, the Quentin R. Mease Community Hospital, which opened its first phase in March 1983. This needed space consists of 50 beds and support services, such as pharmacy, X-ray, and lab facilities, to accommodate patients who may not require the acute medical care given at Ben Taub.

The facilities at Ben Taub are continually being updated. In 1983, it was essential to correct fire and safety code deficiencies and reinforce the employees' garage. At the same time, the patient registration area underwent a necessary remodeling, a blood donor center was added to the front lobby, and the gift shop was expanded. Additional major projects were begun in 1984 and 1985.

Ben Taub is well known for its Category-I emergency and shock/trauma center, which handles approximately three hundred cases a day.

This public hospital offers exceptional medical care by outstanding doctors and nurses. Ben Taub's clinics are always busy, commonly seeing more than 700 outpatients every day. Understanding staff and social workers solve seemingly insurmountable problems with the frequency of miracle workers. Emergencies and acute cases are handled immediately. Elective surgery must be scheduled on a space-available basis. The hospital remains 85 percent occupied at all times.

Ben Taub management and employees communicate the spirit of this institution. It is their understanding that sick people act unnaturally, circumstances may be confusing, and the family is likely to be upset. Their calm reassurance and compassion show a sincere interest in helping others.

Being a major teaching hospital for Baylor, Ben Taub is frequently visited by eminent physicians, lecturers, and educators. Nuclear medicine imaging, computerized axial tomography, ultrasonography, and computerized lab facilities are among its current capabilities. Hemodialysis, cardiac catheterization, and special X-ray procedures are vital parts of patient care.

Specialized training includes programs for chaplain interns, medical technology interns, operating room technologists, graduate nurse anesthetists, as well as counselors in alcohol abuse. Ben Taub also directs area-wide fire department telemetry.

FOOD SERVICE
There are three locations for food service. A coin-operated snack bar, widely used by patients, visitors, and employees, is at the north end of the first floor. Two dining rooms are positioned side by side near the first-floor south entrance. Cafeteria #1 primarily serves full meals, while Cafeteria #2 is for light and short-order meals. Cafeteria #1 is reserved for employees only, while Cafeteria #2 is open to the public from 11:00 AM to 3:00 PM and from 4:45 PM to 6:30 PM.

SHOPPING FACILITIES
A gift shop, staffed by volunteers, is located on the first floor in the lobby near the information booth. It has a variety of gift items, such as greeting cards, plants, cut flowers in vases, jewelry, newspapers, books (new and used), and novelties. Generally open from 10:00 AM to 4:00 PM, Monday through Friday.

RELIGIOUS SERVICES
Ben Taub's chaplains help patients and their families with trauma, emergencies, illnesses, death, and grief. The hospital has an accredited Residency Chaplaincy Program, which gives trainees first-hand experience. Patients are also visited by their own ministers. A chapel is located on the first floor. It offers religious services at different times during the week.

GUIDED TOURS
Tours are given for groups of students from schools and colleges, for physicians and other professionals, and for church organizations, senior citizens, and others. Each tour is tailored to the interests and objectives of the particular gathering.

VOLUNTEERS
Volunteers are helpful in many areas of the hospital. Depending on their skills and interests, they work as ward, staff, and radiology aides; at the information desk; in the gift shop; as receptionists in the surgical intensive care unit, central services, or pediatrics; with the chaplain service; and as patient escorts. Interested applicants may call the Volunteer Department (791-7272), Monday through Friday from 8:00 AM to 4:30 PM.

GENERAL INFORMATION
Ben Taub provides health care for medically indigent persons. Immediate help, counseling, and financial assistance are available through the Social Services Department. Social workers arrange aftercare and discharge planning referrals to public agencies and are knowledgeable about available community resources. They can help with certain limited funds for transportation and prostheses. They are, of course, always ready with emotional support for patients and their families. Social workers are readily accessible in all patient areas. For further assistance, the Social Services Department can be called at 791-7557.

There are three pharmacies at Ben Taub. A large outpatient pharmacy is located at the front of the building. The hospital also has a pharmacy connected with its Pediatric Clinic and another for inpatients.

An old pioneer log cabin museum, rich in historically interesting artifacts, stands in front of Ben Taub. It was built by the Daughters of the Republic of Texas in 1936, when Outer Belt Drive was on the outskirts of the city. The log cabin museum is known for its fireplace, built with stones gathered from homes of such prominent early Texas settlers as Sam Houston. The museum is open on Thursdays from 1:00 PM to 4:00 PM and at other times by appointment.

CHECK-IN/CHECK-OUT
Patient eligibility information is available at 659-2865. In order to fill out records, it is necessary for patients to have the following:
Medicare/Medicaid I.D. card
Military I.D. card if in the U.S. Armed Forces
Social Security number
Drivers' license or personal identification (school record, etc.)

CITY OF HOUSTON DEPARTMENT OF HEALTH AND HUMAN SERVICES
CENTRAL ADMINISTRATION BUILDING

1115 N. MacGregor Dr. (77030)
713 / 222-4288

HOURS
M–F, 8 AM–5 PM
PARKING
Front entrance
RECEPTION
Front lobby

The Department of Health and Human Services, which moved to the Texas Medical Center in 1965, is charged with protecting and promoting healthy living conditions for the people of Houston. Besides offering preventive health services and programs to citizens, this organization must resolve health problems and enforce laws and ordinances dealing with health matters. It also acts as an agency of the state of Texas for lab and vital statistics services.

Houston's Health Department is divided into seven sections, each responsible for programs and activities in a specific health-related area.

The Administrative Support Division establishes and executes programs, services, policies, and procedures for the operation of the Health Department. Planning, budgeting, data processing, personnel management, public information, maintenance, operational services, and security are handled by this section. Administrative Support also encompasses the Office on Aging, which serves as the official agency on aging for Houston and Harris County and administers programs funded by the federal Older Americans Act and the Texas Omnibus Hunger Act. Through subcontracts with private agencies, it provides a wide variety of services to the elderly, including "Meals on Wheels" and meals served in congregate centers.

The Disease Control Division is concerned with investigating and controlling the spread of human and zoonotic diseases. This division includes the Bureau of Vital Statistics, a source of information on births and causes of deaths; the Bureau of Epidemiology, for detection and investigation of possible disease sources and spread; the Bureau of Laboratory Services, which handles analysis of samples and is a reference lab for other governmental agencies; the Bureau of Communicable Diseases, which carries out such programs as TB control, sexually transmitted diseases (STD) control, and immunizations; and the Bureau of Animal Regulation and Care, which handles animal bite cases and the control of zoonotic diseases (human diseases acquired from animals, such as rabies).

The Technical Support Division provides technical assistance in meeting health needs. This section supplies information about Health Department services and prevention of local health problems. It offers patient education at health centers, develops audiovisual aids, interacts with other community health institutions, and conducts training for Health Department staff. Additionally, Technical Support oversees multiservice center operations and manages space for agencies that provide social services to residents of Houston. Also among its responsibilities is recruiting volunteers when needed.

The Personal Health Services Division is the Health Department's clinical unit. This section offers direct medical care, mainly preventive in nature. Personal health services range from family planning for teens and adults to prenatal care, dentistry, and screening for hypertension, diabetes, and cancer. The Emergency Medical Services (EMS) section trains and certifies advanced ambulance technicians. Health care is provided at the city's eight centers, the jail clinic, and other sites in Houston.

The Consumer Health Services Division handles sanitary inspections in retail, wholesale, and institutional food establishments. It provides sanitation training in a food manager's certification program and updates training for the department's inspectors.

The Environmental Pollution Control Division seeks to control air and water quality, noise, and radiation and to ensure a healthy, hazard-free work environment for Houstonians by inspecting, monitoring, and enforcing regulations.

The Environmental Services and Preventive Maintenance Division is responsible for enforcing the city's sanitation ordinances concerning solid waste, weed, and rodent control and tire control standards. Maintenance and repairs for Health Department equipment and vehicles are also performed by this division.

The City of Houston Department of Health and Human Services Central Administration Building houses a complex and diverse number of services that directly affect individuals from a large cross-section of Houston. Employees inside the organization refer to this installation as "Central"; others, outside the system, say "Health Department." No matter what it is called, this facility has devoted, trained professionals who provide invaluable service to citizens citywide.

Healthscope, a quarterly publication of this organization, lists special clinic schedules, advisory council meeting dates, course schedules, and other operational information.

FOOD SERVICE
The Central Administration Building has a cafeteria/lunchroom in the basement. Hot meals are served for breakfast and lunch, 6:30 AM to 4:30 PM, Monday through Friday. A shaded, green area with tables for picnicking is found between the buildings of the Health Department and the University of Houston School of Pharmacy.

GUIDED TOURS
Tours may be arranged by request.

VOLUNTEERS
The Health Department recruits and trains volunteers to serve in all areas of public health. For information, contact the Technical Support Division.

GENERAL INFORMATION
The Health Department offers many social services; to determine eligibility, call 222-4224. Immunizations, Pap smears, maternity services, well-baby exams, family planning, dental care, and tests for diabetes, STD, TB, and sickle cell anemia are some of the individual services provided. The Health Department has a mobile health unit, which reaches those who cannot visit a health center or clinic. The department also investigates animal bites and picks up stray animals.

The Sexual Assault Prevention / Treatment Program (222-4224) helps rape victims with medical and mental care and offers advice on criminal justice matters.

The WIC (Women, Infants, and Children) (526-2026) health care service is set up to ensure that those in need receive supplemental food and learn the basics of proper nutrition.

The Sexually Transmitted Diseases (STDs) program offers confidential examinations. Appointments are made by calling West End Health Center (869-7724), Riverside Health Center (790-0616), or Lyons Health Center (675-7531).

Tuberculosis Control (840-8352) tests for TB and arranges treatment for tuberculosis patients.

Pollen counts are given at certain times during the year by calling 222-4216, and a report of Houston's air quality is available at 795-4994.

1133 M. D. Anderson Blvd. (77030)
713 / 790-1414

PARKING
Garage #3

The Doctors' Club, the only club of its kind in the United States, was founded in 1954 by medical and dental professionals. Located in the Jesse H. Jones Library Building, this private organization caters to a community of private practitioners and officers and academicians of medical and dental schools, hospitals, and clinics throughout Texas, as well as the rest of the country.

The club offers banquet and conference rooms for scientific and educational meetings, along with an elegant dining room and wine cellar. Some seventy-five banquets are held monthly by medical, dental, and professional societies. The Doctors' Club also hosts special events for members, including holiday buffets, dinner theaters, and seminars.

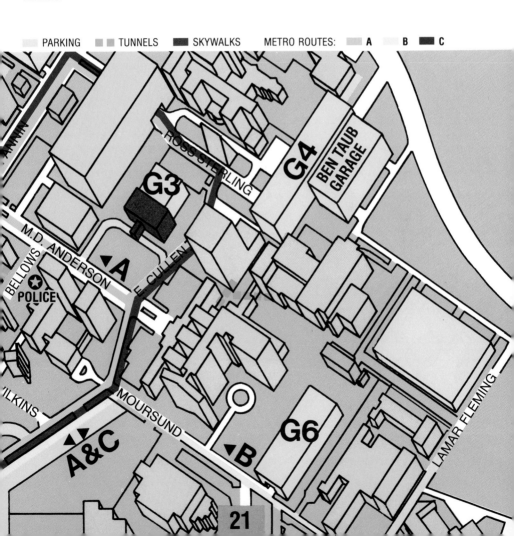

PARKING   TUNNELS   SKYWALKS   METRO ROUTES: A   B   C

HARRIS COUNTY MEDICAL SOCIETY

400 Jesse H. Jones Library Building
1133 M. D. Anderson Blvd. (77030)
713/790-1838
Security: 795-0000 or 790-0656

HOURS
M–F, 9 AM–5 PM
PARKING
Garage #3; short-term meters in front of
building (quarters only)
RECEPTION
Fourth floor

PARKING   TUNNELS   SKYWALKS   METRO ROUTES: A   B   C

The Harris County Medical Society (HCMS) incorporated in 1903. It founded the Houston Academy of Medicine in 1915 and moved its offices, along with the Academy Library, to the Texas Medical Center when the Jesse H. Jones Library Building was completed in 1954.

HCMS, a nonprofit professional association with more than 5,500 physician members, is dedicated to increasing medical knowledge, raising the standard of medical education, and maintaining and advancing the principles of medical practice. Its goals are service to the public and service to the medical profession.

HCMS has been instrumental in the establishment of several important area institutions, such as the Museum of Medical Science. The society led efforts to form the Houston Fire Department Ambulance Service and sponsored the formation of the Gulf Coast Regional Blood Center, as well.

The society offers a free physician referral service (790-1885) to any individual requesting the name of a doctor in a certain specialty or in a specific area of town.

HCMS is involved in focusing public awareness on health. As part of its education program, it provides speakers for hundreds of business, professional, and civic organizations and schools.

To call attention to the problems of driving while intoxicated, HCMS joined the Houston Bar Association in developing a program that included a legislative effort to campaign against drunk drivers and a thirty-minute documentary film to be shown throughout the state of Texas. Doctor-attorney speaker teams have given presentations to many groups.

Because it is committed to upholding professional standards, HCMS investigates grievances and serious patient complaints regarding the medical practice of its member physicians.

A recent activity, the Medication Call-a-thon, paired doctors with an equal number of pharmacists to respond to telephone calls from individuals with questions or concerns about their medications. The group, while not diagnosing or prescribing, provided information about prescriptions and over-the-counter products.

Other community education efforts include the unique Health Adventure health mobile with special displays used to visit schools. HCMS's Auxiliary annually sponsors the Christmas Collection to raise funds for the promotion of better health care and education, to support nursing scholarships, and to benefit the Museum of Medical Science.

2800 South MacGregor Way and Highway
288 (77021)
713/741-5000

HOURS
M–F, 8 AM–5 PM; visiting, 6 PM–8 PM; Sa,
Su, & holidays, 1 PM–3 PM, 6 PM–8 PM
PARKING
Lot across the street
RECEPTION
First-floor lobby

PARKING ■■ TUNNELS ■■ SKYWALKS METRO ROUTES: ■■ A B ■■ C

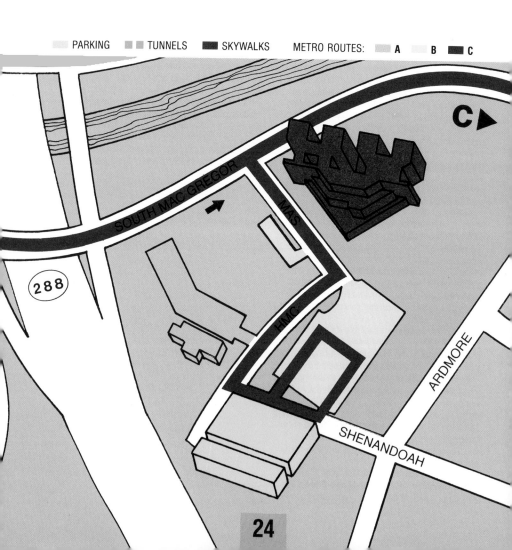

The Harris County Psychiatric Center is a joint state and county psychiatric hospital. The new 250-bed, three-story facility, opened in 1986, is operated by the University of Texas Health Science Center at Houston and is staffed by faculty from UT Medical School's Department of Psychiatry and Behavioral Sciences.

The Texas Department of Mental Health and Mental Retardation, Harris County's Mental Health Mental Retardation Authority, and the University of Texas Health Science Center at Houston cooperated to form this exceptional public hospital to care for the county's mental health needs. The center expects three thousand admissions each year for short- and intermediate-term comprehensive care.

The Harris County Psychiatric Center combines the finest in patient care with education of professionals in treating the mentally ill and research into causes and cures of mental illness. Patients are referred by Harris County's Mental Health Mental Retardation Authority.

Children and adolescents under eighteen years of age are treated for personality disorders, attention-deficit disorders, and difficulties stemming from physical handicaps, child abuse, and psychosomatic problems. Comprehensive treatment is available for adults with personality disorders, affective disorders, and schizophrenia, as well as those with alcohol and substance abuse problems. Geriatric patients receive evaluation and care for emotional, memory, behavioral, and psychosocial problems.

UT Health Science Center's sophisticated equipment, such as the positron emission tomography scanner and magnetic resonance imaging system, make possible investigations into functions of the brain. These new technologies expand the possibilities in development and monitoring individual treatment plans for psychiatric disorders.

GUIDED TOURS
Tours are conducted Tuesdays at 1:15 PM for groups of no more than five people.

VOLUNTEERS
Volunteers are always needed. Contact the volunteer coordinator at 741-7878.

6411 Fannin St. (77030)
713 / 797-4011
Patient information: 797-4130
Security: 797-4000

HOURS
Visiting: 12 noon–9 PM, daily
(minimum age: 12)
Emergency: 24 hours daily (797-4060)

PARKING
Garage #4; limited patient drop-off/pick-up at
Fannin St. entrance; Hermann Professional
Bldg. garage; convenient but expensive lot
near Cullen Pavilion

RECEPTION
Main entrances to Robertson, Jones, and
Cullen pavilions

PARKING   TUNNELS   SKYWALKS   METRO ROUTES: A   B   C

HERMANN PARK

OUTER BELT DRIVE

SOUTH MAIN

HERMANN GARAGE

FANNIN

ROSS STERLING

G3

G4

BEN TAUB GARAGE

M.D. ANDERSON

E. CULLEN

BELLOWS

POLICE

A

C

26

Hermann Hospital was established in 1925 under trust provisions in the will of philanthropist George H. Hermann. This cornerstone institution was the first hospital in the Texas Medical Center. It is owned and operated by the Hermann Hospital Estate and is governed by a board of trustees, whose members donate their services.

While Hermann is a private, teaching, nonsectarian health care facility, it is also a nonprofit community hospital. It is supported solely by money for medical services rendered, donations from individuals and corporations, and foundation grants. It receives no tax money from the city of Houston, Harris County, or the state of Texas.

This tripavilion complex consists of the Hugh Roy and Lillie Cranz Cullen Pavilion, the original hospital built in 1925; the Corbin J. and Wilhelmina C. Robertson Pavilion, finished in 1948; and the Jesse H. and Mary Gibbs Jones Pavilion, opened in 1977. The three interconnected buildings comprise over a million square feet.

As a tertiary care medical institution, accredited by the Joint Commission on the Accreditation of Hospitals, Hermann can care for the most serious cases. Since 1980, it has brought together numerous hospitals into the Affiliated Hospital Systems, to provide support to individual hospitals and the entire group. Hermann employs about three thousand health care and support personnel.

Hermann Hospital's purpose is fourfold. It is committed to providing excellence in health care service and practice in a comprehensive and cost-effective way, meeting community needs with the level and range of services offered, contributing an atmosphere that promotes education and growth of health care personnel, and improving the health of all through research and investigation.

Hermann is the primary teaching hospital for the University of Texas Medical School at Houston. It also serves as a teaching facility for the other members of the University of Texas Health Science Center at Houston.

Hermann is considered a major emergency (Category I) and shock/trauma center for the greater Houston area. Life Flight, its emergency medical air transport helicopter service, carries a physician, a nurse, and complete emergency care to victims of life-threatening incidents within a 150-mile radius of Harris, Galveston, and Jefferson counties. Hermann was the first nonmilitary hospital in Texas to initiate an emergency medical helicopter program. It has become the largest hospital-operated air transport program in the country, with the help of fire departments, police departments and other law enforcement agencies, ambulance companies, physicians, and all the hospitals in the service radius. With Life Flight, chances for survival of critically injured patients are greatly increased.

A helistop was built above the Emergency Center in 1973. To extend the hospital's emergency services, Life Flight was begun in 1976. It started with one helicopter and has expanded to three based at Hermann. Two others are stationed at Baptist Hospital of Southeast Texas, Inc., in Beaumont and at the University of Texas Medical Branch at Galveston.

The Life Flight program includes Life Flight LD (Long Distance), which transports patients all over the world by plane. Life Flight helicopters must be requested by authorized personnel (police or fire departments, ambulance services, physicians, hospitals, industrial safety representatives), but any individual may order Life Flight LD service.

The hospital provides comprehensive care in many specialties. A multidisciplinary team in Hermann's unique Burn Center can deliver treatment for patients with all degrees of burns. Hermann maintains one of the few skin banks in the nation and supplies vitally needed tissues to burn victims.

The unique University Clinical Research Center has been set up at Hermann by UT Medical School. Studies conducted include hypertension, heart disease, obesity, immune disorders, blood clotting, and osteoporosis. This "hospital within a hospital" is a controlled clinical research environment.

The Texas Kidney Institute, opened in 1982, gives extensive care to people with all stages of kidney disease. There are inpatient and outpatient facilities for dialysis, medical, and surgical care. Specialized equipment allows urodynamic studies. More renal transplants are performed at Hermann than at any other hospital in the region. Nearly one hundred people each year find a less restrictive life with a transplanted kidney. The first liver transplant in Houston was performed at Hermann in 1985.

The University of Texas Medical School, a leading researcher with the antirejection drug cyclosporine, and Hermann Hospital have formed a major transplant center. In addition to hundreds of kidney transplants, doctors have performed liver and pancreas transplants.

The Family Center, an obstetric and gynecology service, focuses on family involvement in the birth of a baby. Classes prepare prospective parents and their children for the arrival of a child or sibling. A birthing room allows natural delivery in a home atmosphere.

The Neonatal Care Center provides intensive care for critically ill newborns, as well as intermediate and special care for infants requiring more than routine attention. The Neonatal Inten-

sive Care Unit offers the most advanced equipment and has an outstanding survival rate.

The newly established University Children's Hospital at Hermann is the result of further affiliation with the University of Texas Medical School at Houston and promises to become a leader in providing superior health care to children.

The Children's Center brings a reassuring atmosphere to hospitalized youngsters. Child Life coordinators help children and their families handle fears and uncertainties. Outside the pediatric unit, the hospital has a sunny children's terrace furnished with specially modified playground equipment for ill and injured children.

Hermann Hospital Psychiatric Units deliver diagnosis and treatment to mentally and emotionally disturbed adolescents, adults, and senior citizens.

The hospital is one of the few in the Houston area with complete sexual assault counseling services.

Hermann's Alcohol Problem Treatment Program is a month-long course of treatment, counseling, and rehabilitation for alcoholics. Many patients choose this treatment for themselves, while others seeking help are referred through their jobs.

Hermann Hospital is one of five pioneers to use the enzyme streptokinase to dissolve blood clots, which reduces the risk of permanent heart damage after heart attacks. The Cardiac Catheterization Laboratory, opened in 1982, is equipped to perform this innovative procedure for treatment of heart disease.

Among other noteworthy programs at Hermann are Lifeline, a service that provides immediate help for the elderly, the disabled, and individuals living alone, by linking personal mobile transmitters with Hermann's Emergency Center via telephone; the Sleep Studies Laboratory; and the Gulf States Hemophilia Center, one of only a few diagnosis and treatment centers for hemophiliacs in the United States.

The Hermann Eye Center is known as one of the finest low-vision clinics in the United States. Extremely specialized equipment allows doctors to perform eye surgery and to treat patients with ophthalmologic problems.

A unique Center for Sports Medicine is open for young athletes who want individual medical, psychosocial, and fitness guidance from sports medicine specialists. The center also caters to adult recreational athletes.

A recent affiliation with the Institute for Rehabilitation and Research has established a network of services to benefit patients with severe and disabling injuries or illnesses.

Other noteworthy services include the Cullen Department of Diagnostic Radiology, equipped with computerized tomography (CT scanning), ultrasound imaging, and a treatment system that reduces the amount of radiation delivered to patients and staff by 60 percent over conventional equipment. The ECAT System (emission computed axial tomography), in the Positron Diagnostic and Research Center, is a new method in nuclear medicine imaging that allows physicians to see inside the body without surgery. It will be used for research and diagnosis of diseases, such as stroke and heart attack, before symptoms are noticeable. Hermann recently acquired a powerful magnetic resonance imaging (MRI) system, which poses no radiation hazard because it does not use X rays but produces images of almost photographic detail by means of magnets and radio waves. It is considered a major step in understanding diseases and accurately guiding treatments.

Laboratory Medicine at Hermann has been taken as a model for other facilities in Texas. Diagnostic and administrative procedures, quality control measures, and safety precautions of Laboratory Medicine have been adopted by many other health care institutions.

Day surgery affords a convenient, less expensive way for patients to undergo minor procedures, such as tonsillectomies. Other outpatient services include oral surgery, oncology and radiation therapy, audiology and speech therapy, physical and occupational therapy, dialysis, and treatment for allergy and hemophilia.

Hermann supports several information and emergency hotlines. The hospital also has a physician referral service (797-4300). The Hermann Drug Information Center has a toll-free phone number for physicians and health care professionals in Texas and surrounding states. Using computer data banks, a pharmaceutical staff gathers, evaluates, indexes, organizes, stores, summarizes, and gives out drug information.

LIFE, an acronym for Long-distance Information For Education, offers physicians in Texas and nearby areas toll-free telephone consultation on patient-related problems. Faculty at the University of Texas Medical School at Houston provide information in their specialties.

Hermann also offers services for the deaf. Teletypewriters in three locations enable the deaf to communicate with hospital personnel by telephone. Hearing-impaired inpatients wear special ID bracelets so the staff is alerted to their particular needs.

The Southeast Texas Poison Center is a hotline service operated by Hermann Hospital in cooperation with the University of Texas Medical School at Houston and the Medical Branch at Galveston. Information on poisoning and emergency treatment

is accessible 24 hours a day.

Among the educational programs at Hermann Hospital is the School of Vocational Nursing. Since its beginning in 1956, nearly one thousand students have participated in the one-year nationally accredited course.

The Department of Pastoral Care and Education has a staff of chaplains of many denominations who bring spiritual and emotional support to patients, families, friends, and staff.

FOOD SERVICE
The cafeteria, located on the first floor of the Robertson Pavilion, is open from 6:00 AM to 3:00 AM, daily. Hot and cold meals are served. One guest tray per meal may be ordered and served in a patient's room. Arrangements must be made through the Cashier's Office (Jones Pavilion; 797-4003) at least two hours before delivery. A complimentary birthday cake for a patient may be ordered from the Dietary Department (797-2200) at least one day in advance.

SHOPPING FACILITIES
A gift shop, run by Hermann Hospital volunteers, is located on the first floor of the Jones Pavilion and has a large selection of gifts, magazines, newspapers, paperbacks, candy, plants, and toiletries and rents videos. Open 8:00 AM to 5:00 PM, Monday through Friday; noon to 5:00 PM, Saturday and Sunday.

LIBRARY FACILITIES
A medical staff library is located on the first floor of the Cullen Pavilion. Most departments maintain small libraries with professional reading materials.

RELIGIOUS SERVICES
The Department of Pastoral Care and Education has two facilities for worship: the Mirtha G. Dunn Interfaith Chapel, located in front of the Robertson Pavilion on Ross Sterling Avenue, is open daily from 8:00 AM to 8:00 PM; the Sterling Prayer and Meditation Room, next to the lobby on the first floor of the Cullen Pavilion, is open daily from 6:00 AM to 6:00 PM.

Most denominations are represented. All worship services are open to the public, and some services are broadcast to patients over the hospital's closed-circuit TV channel. Volunteer Services provides escorts for patients who wish to attend. A chaplain is assigned to each patient care unit, and clergy are on call in the hospital, 24 hours daily.

OVERNIGHT ACCOMMODATIONS
Overnight stays by family members depend upon a patient's condition and must be approved by

the nurse in charge of that unit. Night visits can be arranged only for patients in private rooms. A parent may stay the night with a child in children's units. The Patient Relations Department (797-4540) can help with questions about local accommodations.

GUIDED TOURS
Tours of nonpatient areas are conducted on Thursdays, between 8:30 AM and 4:30 PM. A two-week advance reservation is required. Those requesting a tour must be 16 years of age or older.

VOLUNTEERS
The Department of Volunteer Services has openings in all areas of the hospital, during the day, at night, and on weekends. There are many opportunities for the almost two hundred volunteers that involve patient or family contact. Workers help in the Surgical Intensive Care Unit (SICU) family waiting room, assist in the Recovery Room and in the SICU itself, and serve as interpreters through Patient Relations. Volunteers handle the "Care Cart" that visits patients and their families with newspapers, magazines, books, and snacks. There are also volunteer places for bookkeepers, receptionists, file clerks, and in other jobs.

The department has a junior volunteer program for those between the ages of 14 and 17. The senior volunteer program is for those over 18. A commitment of three months is required for volunteers, and they must work a minimum of four hours each week.

GENERAL INFORMATION
The Department of Clinical Social Work (797-4190) gives assistance to patients and their families twenty-four hours a day. The staff offers counseling, referral to community agencies and special resources, and social services.

The Department of Patient Relations also provides many services. Counselors can answer questions about local accommodations and parking or supply an interpreter or a notary public. They help to solve problems, acting as liaison or go-between for patients or families and any doctors, nurses, or hospital sections.

A general pharmacy is available to employees of Hermann Hospital, to the University of Texas Medical School at Houston, and to patients who are being discharged.

Hermann Hospital Speakers' Bureau provides speakers for hundreds of Houston-area organizations, civic groups, clubs, churches, and schools. Talks or discussions include many health-related topics. Speaking engagements are arranged through the Office of Public Affairs (797-4100).

Patients, staff, and visitors may request security escorts to parking areas. Lost items or belongings left behind by patients are kept in the Lost and Found, which may be contacted at 797-2155.

The Hermann Hospital Blood Bank (Robertson Pavilion, ground floor), a district donor site for the Gulf Coast Regional Blood Center, is always seeking volunteer blood donors. A blood donation will result in a credit on a family member's hospital bill. The Blood Bank is open from 10:00 AM to 5:30 PM, Sunday through Thursday.

Contributions to the hospital may be made by contacting the Development Office, Hermann Hospital Estate, or, if the donation is a particular service, by contacting the director/manager of that particular service.

Three quarterly publications, *Horizons, MD Practice,* and *Development Oakline,* present the latest news about the many programs at Hermann.

CHECK-IN/CHECK-OUT
In order to fill out insurance and financial records, it is necessary for you to have the following:
Medicare/Medicaid I.D. card
Blue Cross or other insurance I.D. card
Military I.D. card if in the U.S. Armed Forces
Social Security number
Driver's license

HIGH SCHOOL FOR HEALTH PROFESSIONS

3100 Shenandoah St. (77021)
713/741-2410

HOURS
M–F, 8 AM–4 PM
PARKING
Eastwood Bldg. lot; visitors should get permit
from administration office
RECEPTION
Administration office, first floor

PARKING ■■ TUNNELS ■■ SKYWALKS METRO ROUTES: ■ A ■ B ■■ C

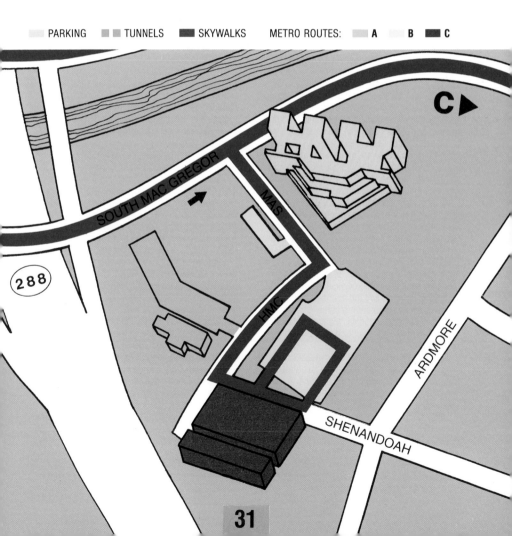

In the early 1970s, Baylor College of Medicine developed a program for a health career high school because of a critical shortage of allied health personnel. After a long period of planning and work by Baylor and the Houston Independent School District (HISD), High School for Health Professions (HSHP) became a reality. This unique school, the first of its kind in the nation, is a part of the prestigious Texas Medical Center. Classes for high school students interested in medical and health careers began at Baylor College of Medicine on Monday, October 2, 1972. Initial enrollment was 45 sophomores chosen from 150 applicants.

HSHP is operated jointly by Baylor's Center for Allied Health Manpower Development and HISD. A committee of individuals from both institutions evaluates and updates courses to meet constantly changing requirements in health care.

HSHP has been housed in the Eastwood Building for Health Careers since 1980. It offers a four-year health-oriented curriculum, health occupational training, and job counseling to give its students the ability to enter a career directly or to continue specialized studies. Many graduates are enrolled in medical school or doctoral studies in medicine.

Although HSHP is part of the "magnet" school program of HISD, it presently also has students from many school districts surrounding Houston. Tuition and bus transportation are provided free to students in the greater Houston area.

HSHP is open to individuals interested in sciences who possess a desire to help people. Acceptance by an admissions committee requires a good school record through eighth grade. Because of the purpose and commitment of those who choose and are chosen by HSHP, attendance and discipline problems are nonexistent.

Pupils receive a specialized education but are expected to meet all academic requirements set forth by the Texas Education Agency and HISD. Although the physical education requirement for grades 10, 11, and 12 has been waived by the state to allow students time to pursue specific interests, the focus on health careers makes lifelong physical fitness a natural part of the overall program. A modern gymnasium gives students an opportunity for gymnastics, weight lifting, volleyball, basketball, and other sports.

The core curriculum centers on traditional academic skills. Electives in foreign languages, advanced mathematics, advanced sciences, and business are offered. As students gain a strong general education, they also participate in health science courses. They are given theoretical training as well as practical experience.

Because of the close association between Baylor College of Medicine and HSHP, students frequently have visiting lecturers from the Baylor faculty. The Texas Medical Center Library, the Houston Academy of Medicine, and Baylor's lab facilities are available for student use. Additionally, HSHP itself has equipment that duplicates medical laboratories, hospitals, and clinics. Students have videotaping capabilities and in-room TV.

An introductory course in health sciences acquaints new students with medical history, ethics, and legal concepts associated with the medical professions.

A health careers course familiarizes sophomores with career opportunities. Students are instructed in anatomy, physiology, and medical terminology. They learn recognition of vital body signs and administration of basic diagnostic and first aid procedures, such as cardiopulmonary resuscitation (CPR).

HSHP juniors investigate health careers in more depth. Classroom instruction is supplemented with experience in labs, hospitals, and clinics, in such courses as patient care, public and environmental health, medical laboratory skills, dental assisting, medical assisting, and medical office education.

The advanced health science course includes the equivalent of first-year college classes in physiology, histology, and microbiology. A licensed vocational nursing program prepares HSHP students for LVN certification within eight months after graduation. Cooperative training offers an option for paid internships in one of five different health fields. Seniors may elect to work as paid interns in a medical laboratory, hospital, dental or medical office, veterinary clinic, or pharmacy.

HSHP has many activities to round out this special high school education. Organizations include the Student Council, Honor Society, and Choir; clubs foster interest in ecology, speech, Spanish, Latin, international culture, chess, and math. There is also an Office Education Association, a Christian Student Union, and such national associations as Future Business Leaders of America and American Field Services.

Health Occupations Students of America has different chapters for special interests. HSHP students hold offices in area clubs in addition to local chapters and have won recognition in numerous competitions.

HSHP undergraduates are encouraged to enter science fairs, literary contests, and other competitive events. Many have been awarded scholarships for higher education.

HSHP has been recognized by the National Science Teachers Association as one of fifty schools in the United States with exemplary science programs. The Rotary Club cited HSHP for the highest attendance record among alternative schools for eight consecutive years.

FOOD SERVICE
A cafetorium is located on the ground floor. Open 11:35 AM to 1:05 PM, Monday through Friday.

LIBRARY FACILITIES
The library, shared with Houston Community College, has an extensive collection of health career books, medical references, and a learning resource center.

VOLUNTEERS
Anyone interested in volunteering to help at HSHP is invited to call Volunteers in Public Schools (626-2950) for information.

400 Jesse H. Jones Library Building
1133 M. D. Anderson Blvd. (77030)
713/790-1838
Security: 790-0656

HOURS
M–F, 9 AM–5 PM
PARKING
Garage #3; short-term meters in front of
building (quarters only)
RECEPTION
Fourth floor

In 1915, the Harris County Medical Society organized the Houston Academy of Medicine. Its primary purpose was to establish a medical library for physicians in Harris County. There was a major effort to construct a building. In 1952, the fund was boosted to $587,000 with a gift of $300,000 from the M. D. Anderson Foundation, which had previously set aside a building site in the Texas Medical Center for a library. Mr. and Mrs. Jesse H. Jones donated money to complete and fully equip the new facility. Ground was broken in 1952 and the Jesse H. Jones Library Building was completed in 1954.

The academy library started with only a few books, but there were almost seventeen thousand volumes in 1949, when an agreement was made with Baylor University College of Medicine to consolidate the two libraries. The library was housed at the medical school until it moved to its present location in the Jesse H. Jones Library Building.

The Houston Academy of Medicine, which shares a board with the Harris County Medical Society, is now one of the financing and governing institutions of the Texas Medical Center Library.

Recent activities have been directed toward providing administrative services to several local chapters of national medical societies. Other efforts are in public health education.

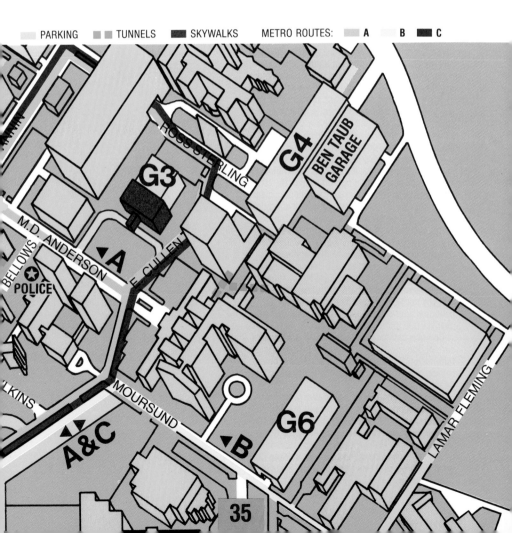

PARKING ■ ■ TUNNELS ■■■ SKYWALKS   METRO ROUTES: ■ **A**   **B** ■■ **C**

Jesse H. Jones Library Building
1133 M. D. Anderson Blvd. (77030)
713/797-1230
Security: 790-1230

HOURS
Library: M–Th, 7:30 AM–12 PM;
F, 7:30 AM–9 PM; Sa, 9 AM–5 PM;
Su, 1 PM–10 PM; holiday schedules vary
Archive (Room 215): M–F, 8 AM–12 noon,
1 PM–5 PM
PARKING
Garage #3; Garage #4; short-term meters in
front of building (quarters only)
RECEPTION
First floor, main entrance

The Houston Academy of Medicine–Texas Medical Center Library is now one of the most highly used medical libraries in the United States. There are some seventeen thousand area users, with almost one thousand visiting daily. The library is unusual in that it is a consortium for and is supported by many separate institutions. Faculty, students, and staff of participating and supporting organizations, as well as the general public, depend on the library for medical information.

The library provides medical references, books, journals, and audiovisual materials. Also housed in the Jesse H. Jones Library Building is the Harris County Medical Archive, established to document the growth and development of medical education, research, and practice in Harris County. The archive provides for the permanent preservation of primary source materials that will be needed by scholars to interpret and understand earlier medical practices, policies, and decisions. Also available at the library are medical information services, manual and computer searches, plus bibliography verification, and interlibrary loans. Its collection contains almost 200,000 volumes, with nearly 3,000 journal subscriptions.

Computerization and expansion are the library's current priorities. A new computer system (Library Information Online) includes an automated union catalog, listing all holdings of the various Medical Center libraries.

The participating institutions, who contribute financial support, appoint members to the board of directors, and help govern the library, include Baylor College of Medicine, Houston Academy of Medicine, Texas Medical Center, Texas Woman's University, University of Texas Health Science Center at Houston, and University of Texas System Cancer Center.

PARKING ▨ TUNNELS ▨ SKYWALKS METRO ROUTES: ▨ A ▨ B ▨ C

The supporting institutions, who contribute to and have use of the library, are City of Houston Department of Health and Human Services, Harris County Hospital District, Hermann Hospital, Institute for Rehabilitation and Research, Memorial Hospital System, Methodist Hospital, Prairie View A&M University College of Nursing, St. Luke's Episcopal Hospital, Shriners Hospital for Crippled Children, Texas Children's Hospital, University of Houston College of Pharmacy, University of Texas Mental Sciences Institute, and Veterans Administration Medical Center.

The library belongs to HARLiC (Houston Area Research Library Consortium). This nonprofit organization was formed for resource sharing and cooperative acquisitions. Member libraries are Houston Academy of Medicine–Texas Medical Center Library, Houston Public Library, Rice University Library, Texas A&M University Library, Texas Southern University Libraries, University of Houston Library, and University of Texas Medical Branch Library (at Galveston).

GUIDED TOURS

Library tours are available for new faculty, clinicians, and staff by appointment. Seminars on the use of the library are given monthly. Information Services has schedules and can answer questions.

VOLUNTEERS

The Friends of the Texas Medical Center Library is an organization whose members include individual Houstonians, faculty, students, and alumni the library's participating and supporting institutions. "The Friends" organization raises money through membership recruitment and donations.

GENERAL INFORMATION

Anyone may use the library, but only library card holders are allowed to borrow materials.

Borrowing privileges at the library are extended to students, faculty, and staff of affiliated institutions. Other qualified persons may obtain a fee-basis badge upon application and approval. The circulation desk has information on services.

Books can be checked out for two-week periods and may be renewed. Bound journals have same-day use only. Nursing journals do not circulate. Unbound journals may be borrowed for two hours. Audiovisual materials are lent for one week and are renewable.

Circulation Services handles circulation of books and journals, book searches and recall, payment for searches and lost books, telephone renewals (for books only), change for copy machines, and locker rentals. Telephone calls are handled through a message board here. Library users will be paged for professional or emergency phone calls.

Information Services handles medical information service, computer search services, bibliography verification, and interlibrary loans. Copies of the Library Handbook are available at this desk. Approximately one hundred automated information services giving access to periodical literature, monographs, dissertations, government documents, and other educational materials are available. Computer searches can be arranged by calling 797-1230.

Newspapers and magazines are found in the library's Leisure Reading area, located on the first floor. Visitors are invited to use this and the Patient Information Collection, located in the reference department. The information collection is designed to help patients and families understand a particular illness and its treatment. Materials are written in easy-to-understand language.

Self-service coin-operated copy machines are available on the second floor. Electric correcting typewriters are also available on the second floor, free on a first-come, first-served basis for authorized library users. Computers are available on the first and second floors for do-it-yourself searching from 8:00 AM to 8:30 PM, Monday through Friday. Ask the librarians about use of the computers.

Educational movies are shown at noon every first and third Thursday. The Medical Center community is invited to bring a sack lunch and attend in Room 007 (street level).

It is difficult to reach the library from the parking garage underneath the Jesse H. Jones Library Building. An elevator carries passengers to street level, where they must exit and walk outside to the front entrance of the library. The elevator goes to other floors but offers no access directly into the library. A second elevator in the lobby, near the front entrance, goes to upper floors but not to the garage.

Handicapped persons who cannot negotiate stairs would need to (a) park in the underground garage; take the elevator to 3 or 4, go up the hall toward the front of the building, and take that elevator downstairs; or (b) arrange for a ramp to be placed over the steps inside, and park in the circular drive in front of the building.

HOUSTON COMMUNITY COLLEGE SYSTEM
HEALTH CAREERS EDUCATION DIVISION

3100 Shenandoah St. (77021)
713/748-8340
Security: 741-2410

HOURS
M–Th, 8 AM–10 PM; F, 8 AM–5 PM
PARKING
Eastwood Bldg. lot; visitors should get permit
from receptionist
RECEPTION
8 AM–10 PM, third floor

PARKING   TUNNELS   SKYWALKS   METRO ROUTES: **A**   B   **C**

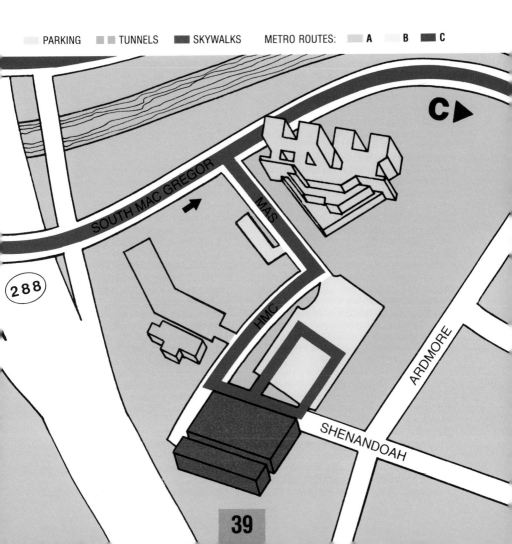

In 1971 voters approved the establishment of a community college as part of the Houston Independent School District (HISD). The Houston Community College (HCC) System, which shares facilities with HISD, offers a wide range of educational opportunities through adult and continuing education, occupational and technical education, and two-year courses transferable to four-year institutions.

HCC Health Careers Education Division, a part of the Texas Medical Center, has fifteen accredited health care programs. Courses vary in length from nine months to two years and include practical experience in labs, hospitals, and clinics along with classroom instruction. The Eastwood school building has extensively equipped laboratories to aid in each phase of training. In-room TV and videotaping capabilities support lab and class activities.

Eleven health career plans require a student to have a high school diploma (or its equivalent), while four offer occupational training to nongraduates. Most classes are taught during the day, but some programs are available in the evening.

Two plans lead to careers in nursing. Trainees have the opportunity to work in Medical Center hospitals. Vocational nursing offers a general nursing education. This one-year course prepares a student to become a licensed vocational nurse (LVN), able to work under the supervision of a registered nurse (RN) or physician. Associate degree nursing graduates are eligible to become registered nurses. Students may enter this two-year class with a high school education and college-level general biology or anatomy and physiology. Some LVNs continue their schooling for an advanced degree.

Dental assisting is a twelve-month, full-time course designed to train students to become cer-tified dental assistants. Hours earned in this program may be credited toward an applied science degree in health technology.

With completion of the two-year medical laboratory technology course, a student is eligible to take the national certifying examination to become a medical laboratory technician. The University of Texas Health Science Center accepts these semester hours in work toward a baccalaureate degree.

Students may earn an associate degree in nuclear medicine technology. This two-year program is concerned with diagnostic and therapeutic use of nuclear materials. Technologists learn safe handling of radioactive chemicals and the operation of sophisticated equipment.

A two-year course of study in radiography leads to an associate in applied science degree, and students can obtain certification with the American Registry of Radiologic Technologists. Registered radiographers are qualified to perform technical procedures using X rays.

The occupational therapy assistant program offers one or two years of study. With completion of the twelve-month course, students are able to apply for certification with the American Occupational Therapy Association. A graduate can find work in hospitals, rehabilitation centers, nursing homes, and schools for the handicapped. An associate in applied science degree is awarded after finishing the second, optional year of academic classwork.

Upon completion of the physical therapist assistant schedule, students may take the state exam to become licensed. Training covers treatment of patients with different diseases and disabilities.

Surgical technicians are instructed in a three-semester course in operating room technology. Graduates learn to assist the surgeon during surgical procedures.

A two-year curriculum in respiratory therapy prepares trainees to become registered respiratory therapists, knowledgeable in respiratory care and in treatments with therapeutic gases, ventilators, medications, and aerosols. They learn bronchopulmonary drainage, cardiopulmonary resuscitation, and other life support measures.

The respiratory therapy technician program is a twelve-month course. Successful completion of the required hours and exam enables students to become certified respiratory therapy technicians.

The health care assistant program is a nine-month class open to those over 18 years of age who are interested in working in a hospital, clinic, lab, or darkroom. Graduates find jobs in blood collecting, central supply, patient escort, and as clinic, medical lab, pharmacy, and darkroom assistants.

A three-semester certificate program in animal health management prepares graduates for jobs in zoos, research labs, veterinary clinics, humane shelters, pet stores, and stables.

Paramedics and emergency medical technicians are trained by the Health Careers Education Division for employment in emergency medical services.

HCC is continually expanding its education program offerings and has recently developed a diagnostic medical sonography course.

A new program has now been approved by the Coordinating Board for Higher Education in which drug and alcohol abuse counselors are trained in a two-year program.

FOOD SERVICE
A cafetorium, shared with HISD's High School for Health Professions, is located on the ground floor. Open 11:35 AM to 1:05 PM, Monday through Friday.

LIBRARY FACILITIES
The library has an extensive collection of health career books, medical references, and a learning resource center.

GUIDED TOURS
Tours are available and may be arranged with the Campus Director at 748-8340.

GENERAL INFORMATION
Complete student services are available through HCC's centrally located Student Service Center at 320 Jackson Hill. The main number is 868-0740. This center services all student needs, offers counseling and guidance, helps in financial aid matters, can give advice on student placement, and has information for veterans.

THE INSTITUTE FOR REHABILITATION AND RESEARCH

1333 Moursund Ave. (77030)
713/799-5000
Clinic: 797-5919
Security: 797-4049

HOURS
Visiting: M–Th, 9 AM–8 PM; F–Su,
9 AM–9 PM
Clinics: M–F, 8 AM–4:30 PM
PARKING
Garage #6; outpatient parking on east side of
building (off Lamar Fleming St.)
RECEPTION
Next to atrium, east side of building

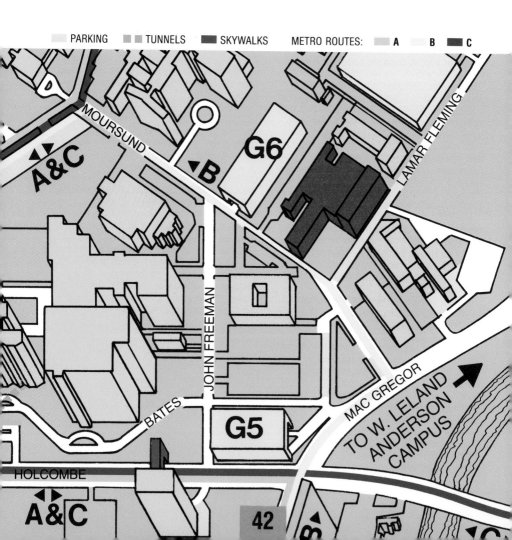

The Institute for Rehabilitation and Research's (TIRR) beginning can be traced to the Southwestern Poliomyelitis Respiratory Center, founded in Houston in 1950. A need for rehabilitation care for many disabling conditions led to the establishment of TIRR in 1959 in the Texas Medical Center. Replacing the polio center, this new institute took that expertise in rehabilitation and applied it to the treatment of patients with a wide range of disabilities caused by illness and injury.

Today TIRR offers restorative services to people of all ages. (The institute has the only comprehensive pediatric rehabilitation program in Texas.) Complete rehabilitation is provided for persons with disabling conditions, from weakness or paralysis to loss of limbs, breathing impairments, and multiple handicaps. Comprehensive care includes medical, psychological, social, and vocational help. Specialized treatments are available for arthritis, stroke, birth defects, circulatory system diseases, pulmonary diseases, multiple sclerosis, muscular dystrophy, neuromuscular and skeletal diseases, polio-related problems, fractures, orthopedic problems, lower extremity and back pain, scoliosis, spinal cord injuries, brain injuries, amputations, hemiplegia, paraplegia, and quadriplegia.

A multidisciplinary team of health professionals directs each TIRR treatment center and program. The group, headed by a physician, decides and monitors the appropriate care for individual patients, from admission to discharge and follow-up.

Disabled patients are taught how to compensate for physical limitations so they may lead productive, satisfying lives. Discharge planning and guidance in the use of community resources help prepare patients for a successful return home.

TIRR is an affiliate of Baylor College of Medicine. It is known worldwide as a pioneer and leader in rehabilitation medicine and is recognized for the expertise of its staff, its exceptional programs, excellent results, and the caring and hope it imparts. TIRR has an affiliation agreement with the Methodist Hospital Health Care System and the Hermann Hospital Estate to coordinate specialized attention for physically disabled persons.

TIRR's programs include service, research, and education. Research brings new information and improves the effectiveness of service and aids decisions on service selection. Education spreads new knowledge and technology.

TIRR has most, if not all, benefits of a general hospital. Rehabilitation services include the Orthotics Department, which creates and constructs devices that assist movement or prevent deformity. Designs incorporate an externally powered hand device that enables paralyzed fingers to hold objects and use utensils, and a lightweight, functional plastic leg brace. The Rehabilitation Engineering Center, using the latest technology, has developed a stand-up wheelchair for children and an environmental control unit, among other items.

Other departments include Clinical Neurophysiology, a unique research and service department providing comprehensive evaluation and the latest in treatment for spasticity and pain and for restoring motor function. The Clinical Neurophysiology Department makes use of a cybex machine for muscle testing, a minicomputer system, electrical stimulators, and devices for recording neuromuscular activity. TIRR's Urology Lab is also unique with its microcomputer-based urodynamic system.

The institute has established a model postpolio project, which aids survivors of paralytic polio who are experiencing new symptoms thirty or forty years after disease onset. Victims of multiple sclerosis (MS) are finding help through the recent addition of an MS clinic.

The 1984 completion of its expansion program added almost 20,000 square feet to the existing facility, raising inpatient bed capacity by 25 percent.

FOOD SERVICE
A cafeteria is open daily, 7:30 AM to 9:30 AM for breakfast and 11:45 AM to 1:30 PM for lunch. There is also a snack bar.

SHOPPING FACILITIES
TIRR has a gift shop, the Korner Store, run by volunteers, selling newspapers, magazines, and books, among other items. The hours vary, so check at the shop.

LIBRARY FACILITIES
There is a medical library with references for staff and patient use. This Information Services Center contains many volumes of rehabilitation material. It serves both TIRR and the University of Texas Speech and Hearing Institute (where it is housed).

RELIGIOUS SERVICES
There are weekly nondenominational services for patients.

GUIDED TOURS
Tours may be arranged by calling the Public Relations office (797-5235) at least one week in advance.

VOLUNTEERS
Volunteers perform valuable services for patients and hospital staff. They help in many areas: at information and reception desks, in offices, in the greenhouse, and in the gift shop. Volunteers assist with patients and carry out a shampoo program. They operate a coffee cart, have plant and bake sales, and organize other projects to raise funds for TIRR. More volunteers are always needed. Additional information is available from the director of volunteers at 797-5225.

GENERAL INFORMATION
Each patient admitted to TIRR is assigned a team of health professionals directed by a physician and comprised of a rehabilitation nurse, occupational therapist, physical therapist, and social worker. Professionals from other disciplines, such as respiratory therapy, orthotics, and vocational services, join the team as needed. The social worker coordinates the group's services to see that each patient gets individualized care. Patients learn to compensate through rehabilitation for physical limitations so they may lead productive and satisfying lives. The social worker plans the discharge and arranges for use of community resources to ensure a successful return home.

TIRR's pharmacy is open to the general public as well as patients and staff. It is open Monday through Friday and has limited hours on Saturday.

Outpatient services available include physical therapy, orthotics, occupational therapy, vocational services, social work, laboratory, radiology services, and driver training.

The statue *Prometheus Unbound* stands in front of the institute as a symbol of rehabilitation. Prometheus, a mythological Greek god, pitied the fact that mortals were made of clay. He stole from the gods a fire capable of endowing humans with the ability of artistic creation. Consequently, Prometheus was put to extreme torture by Zeus, doomed to be chained forever to an inaccessible rocky crag. Hercules released Prometheus from his chains. Similarly, TIRR works to release handicapped persons from the chains of disability.

THE INSTITUTE OF RELIGION

1129 Wilkins St. (77030)
713/797-0600
Security: 795-0000

HOURS
M–F, 8:30 AM–5 PM
PARKING
Garage #1; surface lot across street
RECEPTION
First floor, main entrance

PARKING   TUNNELS   SKYWALKS   METRO ROUTES: A   B   C

The Institute of Religion was chartered in 1955 in response to requests from the medical community. Physicians, nurses, administrators, and chaplains in the Texas Medical Center joined with the Council of Churches of Greater Houston to fill a need for tending spiritual and emotional health while treating the physical person.

The institute was housed in temporary quarters in the Jesse H. Jones Library Building until 1960, when its present four-story home was completed. The structure, with its soaring tower, is set in a shaded, parklike area. Facilities include offices, classrooms and assembly halls.

The institute is an interfaith center for graduate and continuing education and research in pastoral ministry, religion and health, and ethics in medicine. It has provided leadership in medical, nursing, and allied health education by emphasizing the close relationship of emotional, spiritual, and physical health. It offers a "wholistic" approach to modern health care, encouraging treatment of the whole human. It is committed to being a unifying force in tending to the spiritual as well as the physical well-being.

The institute affords learning opportunities for health care workers, religious personnel, and concerned lay people who want to minister more effectively to patients and their families in medical crisis periods of illness, injury, and death. Thousands of men and women of every major religious denomination from all over the world have participated in, and contributed to, the various studies.

Educational programs include theology and ethics, a unique course and the first of its kind in the United States. It focuses on the relationship of moral issues with health care and examines such topics as ethics in human and biomedical re-

search, community and family medicine, genetic engineering, and concerns of the dying.

In 1982, a Center for Ethics, Medicine, and Public Issues was formed in conjunction with Baylor College of Medicine and Rice University. The center offers continuing education classes, seminars, and lectures to practicing physicians, medical and nursing students, and religious and lay members of the community.

Pastoral education programs are given for the many student chaplains in Medical Center hospitals, Houston's clergy, and lay persons. Besides a formal curriculum, the institute sponsors classes and lectures. "Equipping Laypeople for Ministry," a four-day course of seminars and workshops, makes workable the concept that lay congregational members can assist the clergy in caring for the ill. The institute's innovative project covers all aspects of pastoral ministry, from theological origins to home and hospital visits to instructing additional volunteers. The Institute Forum and the Parker Memorial Lectures present many outstanding speakers on theology, ethics, medicine, and ministry.

JOSEPH A. JACHIMCZYK FORENSIC CENTER
OFFICE OF THE MEDICAL EXAMINER OF HARRIS COUNTY

1885 Old Spanish Trail (77054)
713/796-9292 (24 hours daily)
Security: 795-0000

HOURS
M–F, 8 AM–5 PM
PARKING
Beside building
RECEPTION
Entrance lobby

PARKING ░░ TUNNELS ▓▓ SKYWALKS ■■ METRO ROUTES: ░░ A ░░ B ■■ C

The Office of the Medical Examiner of Harris County became a Texas Medical Center member institution in 1983 and continues a well-established trend of locating city and county health-related facilities inside the Medical Center.

Housed in the Joseph A. Jachimczyk Forensic Center of Harris County, the 39,500-square-foot building has been constructed to allow for the addition of three floors when needed at a later date.

This facility ends over a quarter of a century of nomadism for the Medical Examiner's Office, which has shared space in the Criminal Courts building, the Center Pavilion Hospital, the old dental school building, the original Jefferson Davis Hospital, Ben Taub Hospital, and the Citizen's Savings building downtown. During this time, the labs, morgue facilities, and administrative offices were all too often housed in separate locations.

Based on the concept of being a place where those who have died teach and help the living, the new building offers complete forensic capabilities. The morgue area—with a pair of refrigerated vaults; five autopsy suites, each with specially designed skylights for maximum natural illumination; X-ray and photography rooms; and a classroom— is linked by wide, well-lit corridors.

The first floor also contains a bright reception and lobby area, clerical offices, public telephones, and a family viewing room intended to ease some of the pain inherent in a sad moment by making as humane as possible the ordeal of identifying the remains of someone close. The use of closed-circuit TV is an innovation that allows family members to view the deceased, if they wish, from a remote position. The second and third floors contain offices and forensic laboratories.

Dealing with the dead is a vital function in our society. Fewer individuals will literally get away with murder if the medical examiner investigating the cause and manner of death is competent and has good facilities. The new Forensic Center of Harris County provides ideal working conditions for a trained, dedicated team of pathologists, toxicologists, histotechnologists, and key support staffers. What is learned from study in this facility will benefit the citizens of Houston and Harris County while offering increased knowledge of techniques and skills to other forensic medicine centers throughout the country.

THE METHODIST HOSPITAL

6565 Fannin St. (77030)
713/790-3311
Patient Information: 790-2578
Security: 790-4373

HOURS
Visiting: 9 AM–9 PM, daily (minimum age: 14)
Emergency: 24 hours daily (790-2245)

PARKING
Garage #1; surface lot across from main entrance; valet parking at Fannin entrance and at main entrance of Neurosensory Center, 9 AM–9 PM

RECEPTION
Bertner Ave. entrance and Fannin St. entrance

PARKING   TUNNELS   SKYWALKS   METRO ROUTES: A   B   C

The Methodist Hospital is a large complex, consisting of four main centers: The Methodist Hospital, Main Building, is located between Bertner Avenue and Fannin Street. It is connected by tunnel, covered walkway, and skywalk to the Fondren and Brown buildings and the Alkek Tower. A skywalk, across Fannin Street, leads to the Scurlock Tower building. The central Fondren-Brown-Alkek building is also connected by walkway to the Neurosensory Center, located at Fannin Street and M. D. Anderson Boulevard.

Methodist Hospital is not only the largest hospital in Houston but also the largest Methodist hospital in the world. It is a private, internationally known, nonprofit corporation committed to offering excellence in patient care, research, and teaching.

Methodist was established in 1924 as a seventy-bed community general hospital. In 1951, it moved from its facilities near downtown Houston to the developing Texas Medical Center. Upon completion of its current modernization and expansion program in 1988, which includes a ten-story patient tower, and a twenty-four-story professional office building, the number of beds will exceed fifteen hundred.

Methodist Hospital has long been famous for its innovations in cardiovascular surgery and is the surgical base of famed heart surgeon Dr. Michael E. DeBakey. In affiliation with Baylor College of Medicine, the hospital has developed a comprehensive, multiorgan transplant program that can accommodate heart, heart-lung, kidney, cornea, liver, and bone marrow transplants.

The hospital's reputation as a leader and forerunner in medical innovations that are now considered routine has attracted worldwide scientific and public attention. Staff physicians are known for

their contributions in treatment and research in many fields.

Methodist is the primary private adult teaching hospital for Baylor College of Medicine. Staff physicians are on the Baylor faculty, and Baylor department chairmen are chiefs of equivalent services at the hospital. Baylor and Methodist have had a close association since 1950, jointly funding research projects and building facilities within Methodist's complex.

The affiliation of Methodist with educational institutions promotes superior patient care through research and education. Teaching is emphasized for its contributions to high medical standards. Investigation and instruction in almost every discipline of medical science are available for training future professionals.

Many academic programs are offered by the hospital itself and through its affiliations with other institutions, such as Baylor, University of Texas Dental School, University of Houston, Texas Woman's University, University of Texas Health Science Center, Houston Baptist University, and St. Thomas University. The hospital is also affiliated with Washington University in St. Louis, Missouri.

The Neurosensory Center focuses on ear, nose, and throat disorders, as well as audiology, eyesight, neurological, and neuromuscular diseases. Work has led to new treatments for stuttering and sleep disorders. Also at the center is the Jerry Lewis Neuromuscular Disease Research Center, funded by the telethon to study MS (multiple sclerosis), cerebral palsy, muscular dystrophy, ALS (amyotrophic lateral sclerosis), and more-rare neuromuscular diseases.

The Blue Bird Circle Clinic for Pediatric Neurology uses a team approach (neurologists, pediatricians, psychologists, and social workers) to help children with neurological disorders. Patients from all over the world are referred to the clinic, which is supported and partially staffed by a volunteer group, the Blue Bird Circle.

The hospital is recognized for its research in preventive medicine. Investigations into physical and behavioral sciences, as well as health economics, are being conducted at the Sid W. Richardson Institute for Preventive Medicine. The institute teaches patients and the community how life-style changes can lead to healthier, longer, higher-quality lives.

About half of Methodist's patients are Houstonians, but each year there are representatives from all fifty states and more than sixty foreign countries. Approximately 40,000 patients are admitted annually, and well over 600,000 outpatient procedures are performed each year. With completion of the new patient tower in 1988, the number of operating rooms will rise from sixty-four to seventy-five.

There are four CT scanners at the hospital, three linear accelerators, and two cobalt units. In addition, two MRI units have been installed, which produce images by use of magnets and radio waves instead of X rays.

Methodist was one of the first hospitals in the United States to install a lithotripter, which can take the place of surgery in removing kidney stones. In this process, hydrosonic (underwater shock) waves break up stones so they may be excreted.

Methodist's state-of-the-art technology also includes advanced anesthesia monitoring equipment; thirteen lasers, including an endo-laser for microsurgery and a krypton laser; extensive microsurgery capabilities; and extensive facilities for diagnostic cardiac procedures.

The mission of Methodist Hospital is to provide the best patient care in the world and be the best service organization anywhere. Toward this end, the hospital is noted as an innovator in patient services and provides such amenities to its patients and visitors as direct admission, valet laundry and parking services, doormen, bellmen, and concierge services.

FOOD SERVICE
Methodist Hospital (Main Building) has a cafeteria for employees, staff, and visitors on the first floor. It serves breakfast from 6:30 AM to 9:30 AM, lunch from 11:30 AM to 2:00 PM, and dinner from 4:00 PM to 7:00 PM. The Fondren Building has a snack bar on the first floor open 10:00 AM to 3:00 AM, daily. The Neurosensory Center has a snack bar on the ground floor near the M. D. Anderson Boulevard entrance open Monday through Friday, 6:00 AM to 9:00 PM.

Chez Eddy is an elegant, low-cholesterol gourmet restaurant located on the fourth floor of Scurlock Tower. It also offers a take-out lunch service and is open for dinner (call 790-6474). The restaurant is closed Sunday and holidays. Other snack bar/salad/sandwich shops are in Scurlock Tower on the second level.

SHOPPING FACILITIES
A gift shop, operated by the Women's Auxiliary, is on the first floor near the Fannin Street entrance in the Main Building. It has a large selection of gifts, clothing, lingerie, magazines, paperbacks, newspapers, and so on. Open 9:00 AM to 7:00 PM, Monday through Friday; 9:00 AM to 5:00 PM, Saturday; 1:00 PM to 5:00 PM, Sunday.

The Scurlock Tower has a variety of gift, spe-

cialty, uniform, surgical, and optical stores, a travel agency, a beauty/barber shop, a pharmacy, and a bank.

LIBRARY FACILITIES
The hospital has over thirty departmental libraries and collections located in six different buildings. The Ellard M. Yow Library, on the first floor of Methodist's Main Building, is the general library for the complex. Each of the libraries has specific hours and policies, but most limit their use to hospital personnel.

Notable among several departmental libraries is the Cullen Eye Institute Library located on the second floor of Methodist's Neurosensory Center. It is for use by staff and students, but anyone with a demonstrated need for ophthalmological information may use the library.

RELIGIOUS SERVICES
Chaplains are available at the hospital during usual business hours, but are on call 24 hours a day. Patients may request a chaplain through their nurses. Nurses will also respond to a request for a Catholic priest or a rabbi. Clergy from other denominations can be reached through the Chaplains' Office.

Wiess Memorial Chapel has been temporarily relocated to the first floor of the Fondren-Brown buildings. Entry is near the main elevator lobby.

Volunteers are available to help patients get to services in the chapel. Patients may make arrangements through their nurses. The Protestant service is held at 10:00 AM on Sunday, with Catholic mass at 11:00 AM. For more information on services, call the Chaplains' Office at 790-2381.

OVERNIGHT ACCOMMODATIONS
A family member who would like to stay with a patient may request a cot from the nursing unit on the floor. This service, however, is restricted to private rooms.

GUIDED TOURS
Group tours of Methodist Hospital are conducted by appointment. Those interested should call the Public Affairs Department at 831-2966 as far in advance as possible. The number that can be accommodated is limited. Many reservations are made a month in advance, and tours are given on a first-call, first-served basis.

VOLUNTEERS
The hospital has three volunteer programs:
1. The Women's Auxiliary to The Methodist Hospital was founded in 1928 to promote fellow-

ship and service among Methodist women. The Auxiliary owns and staffs the Roberta Powell Dwyer Memorial Gift Shop (in Methodist's Main Building near the Fannin Street entrance, 790-2587).

2. The Blue Bird Circle, organized in 1923, established the Blue Bird Seizure Clinic at Methodist in 1949. In 1977, the clinic was renamed the Blue Bird Circle Clinic for Pediatric Neurology and moved to the Alice and David C. Bintliff Blue Bird Building in the Neurosensory Center. Every year more than four hundred Blue Birds volunteer close to 45,000 hours in the clinic and three fund-raising shops.

3. The Methodist Hospital Service Corps, founded in 1947, donates thousands of volunteer hours in the admitting office, in the chapel, at information desks, with the book cart, in intensive care waiting rooms, in patient care areas, in surgery, at the doctors' coffee bar, and in visiting patients.

Those interested in joining a volunteer group should contact the Volunteer Activities Office at 790-3351.

GENERAL INFORMATION

With their physician's approval, patients may use the Institute for Preventive Medicine Health and Fitness Club, located on the fourth floor of the Scurlock Tower. The facilities include an indoor jogging track, sauna, whirlpool, stationary cycles, treadmills, and weight equipment, plus volleyball, basketball, and racquetball.

A barber shop is located in Methodist's Main Building, first floor. It is open to patients, visitors, and employees for haircuts, shaves, and shoe-shines. Patients may arrange through their nurses to have the barber come to their rooms. A beauty shop is located on the second floor of the Scurlock Tower. It is open to patients, visitors, and employees. Banking and retail services are available in the Scurlock Tower, on the first and second floors.

Medical social workers (Social Services) at 790-3116 are available to help patients, families, and visitors with most problems.

Interpreters can be arranged by calling International Patient Services at 790-5696.

The Scurlock Tower Pharmacy, located on the second floor of Scurlock Tower, fills prescriptions and sells other medications, cosmetics, and personal grooming items. It is open from 8:00 AM until 6:00 PM, Monday through Friday.

Hospital security staff and off-duty Houston Police Department officers routinely patrol the grounds and all buildings. The Security Department monitors at all times a sophisticated system of closed-circuit TV cameras. Patients, staff, and visitors may ask for security representative escorts to parking areas. The Security Department also keeps a Lost and Found.

Methodist presently has three major publications: *Happenings* is an in-house newsletter for employees, *Medical Staff* is an in-house newsletter for the medical staff, and *The Journal* is a quarterly magazine that is distributed throughout the hospital and mailed to interested people.

The mosaic mural at Methodist's Fannin Street entrance is called *The Extending Arms of Christ*. It was designed by artist Bruce Hayes and was constructed in Florence, Italy, of more than 1.5 million pieces of mosaic glass. The artwork, installed in 1963, is divided into three main sections, which suggest the importance of medicine and religion in our past and future. Christ, superimposed upon the hospital's Wiess Memorial Chapel, is the central figure.

CHECK-IN/CHECK-OUT

As a special convenience to patients, Methodist has established a pre-admission procedure, in which all required information is gathered before the admission date, enabling the patient to be admitted directly to the hospital room.

There are two admitting offices: the Main Building Admitting Office, located on the first floor of the Main Building, and the Neurosensory Admitting Office, located on the ground floor of the Neurosensory Building. The admitting physician will know which office is appropriate.

At preregistration, the hospital will require personal data and employer information (if applicable) on both the patient and the person who is financially responsible for the hospital stay. The name of a third-party contact will also be requested. A patient who is insured will need to know:

The name of the insurance company
The name of the company (group) that is insured
Policy, certificate and/or group number
Social Security number of the person insured
Effective date of the policy
Address to which claims should be mailed
For preregistration information, call 790-2042. Out-of-town patients can call collect.

THE NEW AGE HOSPICE OF HOUSTON

Office
6205 Almeda Rd. (77021)
713/467-7423

HOURS
M–F, 8:30 AM–5 PM

Inpatient facility
St. Anthony Center
6301 Almeda Road (77021)
713/748-5021
HOURS
Visiting: 24 hours daily
PARKING
Across from main entrance to St. Anthony
Center (requires 4 quarters—change
available at front desk)
RECEPTION
St. Anthony lobby

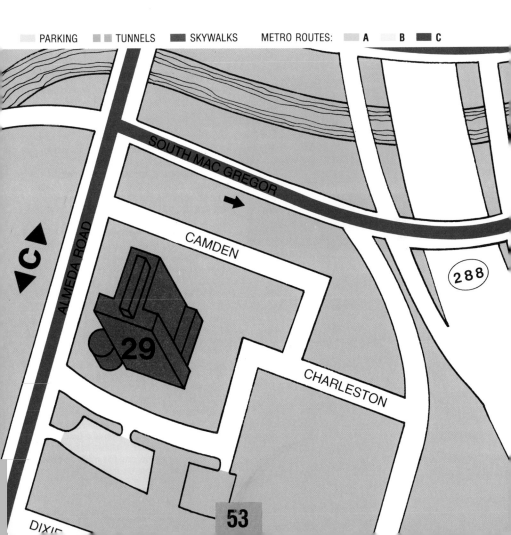

PARKING ▪▪ TUNNELS ▪▪ SKYWALKS METRO ROUTES: ▪▪ A ▪▪ B ▪▪ C

The New Age Hospice is dedicated to helping persons with terminal illnesses. Its goal is to improve the quality of a patient's last few weeks or months of life. Currently quartered in the St. Anthony Center, the hospice is a separate organization and operates in conjunction with Texas Medical Center facilities.

Many think of a hospice as a nursing home where a person goes to die. The hospice, however, is a program committed to the living. It strives to give value to a terminally ill patient's remaining days and to lend support to family members during the illness and after death.

Unlike hospital care, which is directed toward a cure, hospice medical services are aimed at relieving pain and keeping patients comfortable but alert and in control. After that, the psychological, spiritual, and social needs of patients and their families are addressed.

Hospice treatment is notable for its return to fundamental nursing skills and can best be defined as "intensive caring." Each patient and family has different problems during this time of crisis. Enhancing the quality of life requires a great deal of ingenuity, flexibility, and hard work on the part of the hospice team.

Home care is provided through visits by a physician, registered nurse, social worker, chaplain, physical therapist, health aide, or trained volunteer. A physician and nurse are on call 24 hours daily. When care at home is not feasible, short-term inpatient care is available.

Reasons for admission to the inpatient facility vary from the need for symptom control to unsafe home environment, inability to travel back home, and imminent death. When admission becomes necessary, the physician-directed interdisciplinary team offers individualized care in a homelike atmosphere. Patients are encouraged to bring familiar possessions to brighten their rooms. Family members are permitted unlimited visiting hours and may join with others in family rooms. The hospice's intention is to keep patients comfortable, not prolong life with invasive procedures.

The New Age Hospice is a nonprofit organization that provides care regardless of a patient's financial status. Services may also be covered by Medicare, Medicaid, and medical insurance. Most patients are from Harris County, but others may be admitted at the discretion of the director.

Anyone may refer a patient to the New Age Hospice. The patient cannot be admitted, however, until his or her personal physician has given consent, the hospice physician has made an examination and found the referral appropriate, the family has agreed to cooperate, and the patient has signed a consent form.

Corporate and personal contributions enable funding of home care services and an inpatient facility. The New Age Hospice of Houston joined the Texas Medical Center in December 1983.

FOOD SERVICE
The Hogan Dining Room on the first floor of St. Anthony Center offers lunch and dinner. Open 11:30 AM to 12:30 PM, 5:30 PM to 6:30 PM daily. Friends and family may purchase tickets to join patients for meals. A cafeteria serves hot lunches Monday through Thursday, from 11:00 AM to 12:30 PM, and a snack bar has sandwiches. Sandwiches are also available in the gift shop.

SHOPPING FACILITIES
A gift shop in the lobby is staffed by volunteers of St. Anthony Center's Ladies Auxiliary. It is open daily, from 10:00 AM to 3:00 PM.

LIBRARY FACILITIES
The hospice has a library for use by staff and volunteers at the home care office. Magazines, books (regular and big print), and talking book machines for the blind or visually handicapped are provided for patients by St. Anthony's Volunteer Department.

RELIGIOUS SERVICES
A chapel on the first floor is open for meditation, and services are held regularly. A priest and a chaplain are on staff at St. Anthony Center and may be reached through the Pastoral Care Department (748-5021).

OVERNIGHT ACCOMMODATIONS
Visiting at the inpatient facility is permitted twenty-four hours a day. While arrangements can be made for family members to spend the night, the number staying may be limited because of room size.

VOLUNTEERS
Volunteers are an integral part of the hospice team. Some contribute office work, while many are involved in direct care, spending time with patients and families in their homes. Bereavement follow-up is another important part of their services. Volunteers receive twenty hours of special training before being assigned to patient services. Sessions are held at different intervals during the year. Contact the coordinator of Volunteer Services for more information (467-7423).

GENERAL INFORMATION
Social services depend on the individual needs of patients and their families and are provided by staff members with master's degrees in social work.

Assistance for family members does not end at the time of death but continues afterward. Support groups for those who have lost a family member are sponsored as a part of the hospice's bereavement program.

A speakers bureau exists for groups interested in learning more about the New Age Hospice. Information may be obtained from the hospice office.

6436 Fannin St. (77030)
713/797-0722
Security: 790-9171

HOURS
M–F, 8 AM–5 PM
PARKING
Beside building
RECEPTION
First floor lobby

Prairie View A&M University, part of the Texas A&M System, was established as a land-grant college in 1891. The College of Nursing started in 1918 with a two-year curriculum and extended its program to three years in 1928. Soon after, the school formed its first off-campus affiliation with Jefferson Davis Hospital in Houston. By 1948, students received their clinical training in several hospitals in surrounding communities.

A clinical branch was established in Houston in 1968, and the college settled into its first permanent facility, located in the Texas Medical Center, in August 1982. That same year, the College of Nursing became a member of the Medical Center. The college provides health care education and medical resources to students at institutions in the Medical Center, in the Harris County Hospital District, at the Harris County Health Department, and at the Veterans Administration Hospital.

Since its beginning, the college has undergone many changes. Its curriculum has been regularly evaluated and revised in accordance with accreditation standards and constituent needs. The nursing program has two levels of entry: one for registered nurses, the other for high school graduates, including transfer students. The R.N. entry level allows students to study part-time and build upon previous education. In 1979, the school instituted a program for registered nurses who wish to complete their baccalaureate degree in nursing.

Beginning nursing students receive their first two years of education at Prairie View A&M University in Prairie View. Upon completion of basic studies, students continue clinical instruction in Houston. Transfer students from other colleges, universities, and community colleges are reviewed for entry into the Clinical Division after completion

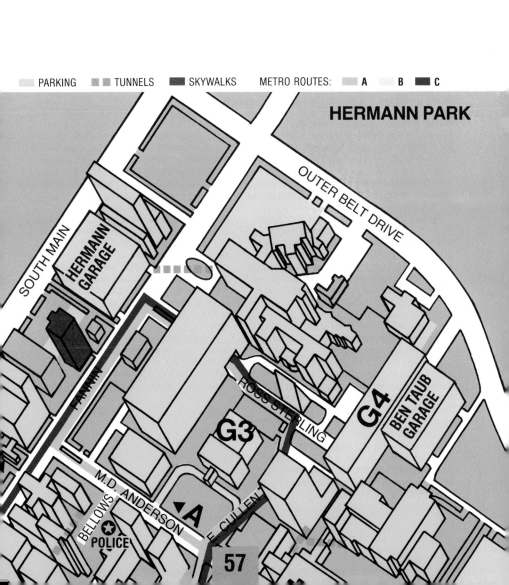

PARKING ■■ TUNNELS ■■ SKYWALKS METRO ROUTES: ■■ A ■■ B ■■ C

HERMANN PARK

OUTER BELT DRIVE

SOUTH MAIN

HERMANN GARAGE

FANNIN

ROSS STERLING

G4

BEN TAUB GARAGE

G3

M.D. ANDERSON

E. CULLEN

BELLOWS

▲A

★ POLICE

57

of sixty-eight semester credit hours of course prerequisites.

The philosophy of Prairie View's nursing program is to provide a liberal education for its students and to prepare beginning practitioners of professional nursing. The program is committed to teaching, research, and community service. In addition to nursing theory and practice, a broad base of studies includes instruction in the humanities as well as behavioral and natural sciences. The college's objective is to instill a sense of accountability and commitment to nursing leadership, research, health promotion, and health maintenance. The legalities and ethics of practice within a professional framework are also addressed.

The college facility offers a modern and spacious educational environment. The quality of instruction is enhanced by state-of-the-art computer technology and laboratory resources. A dedicated faculty contributes to a well-rounded learning experience.

Over three hundred students are enrolled in the bachelor of science degree program. Graduates are eligible to apply to the National Council Licensure Examination for Registered Nurses for license to practice nursing in the state of Texas. In addition, the school recently received continuing accreditation through 1989 from the National League for Nursing.

As the school grows and pursues new directions, it strives to strengthen existing programs and to develop new ones. Plans are underway for graduate studies to prepare nurses in selected specialties. In-depth continuing education courses are taught for registered nurses who wish to gain expertise and certification in the care of the aged. The Clinical Division is being expanded to include more continuing education courses as a service to the community. Certain needs in the field of nursing have been identified and are being addressed, such as nursing research.

Basic and advanced skills laboratories allow students to gain proficiency in nursing skills. The Basic Skills Laboratory is designed as an eighteen-bed hospital unit and offers a simulated hospital training experience. These two practice labs are equipped with the latest in critical care equipment and computer technology. It is envisioned that the Advanced Skills Laboratory will become a model for critical care instruction in nursing education. The college is expanding and equipping its new facility to provide for projected increases in enrollment.

LIBRARY FACILITIES
The college has a Learning Resources Center, which includes a library and a media center. The center is an extension of the Prairie View A&M University W. R. Banks Library and offers selected references and health professions literature.

GUIDED TOURS
Individuals and community and school groups may make arrangements for tours and career awareness sessions through the Office of the Dean.

VOLUNTEERS
The school is developing a volunteer service. Nursing alumni are active in assisting with tutorial services and special events, such as pinning, capping convocations, and other ceremonies.

GENERAL INFORMATION
Students are encouraged to participate in student government, cultural programs, sports, fraternities, and sororities on the main Prairie View campus (about 40 miles away). Group discussions, formal receptions, noon buffets, plays, talent shows, and many extracurricular activities are offered at the Houston Clinical Center. Transportation is provided to the main campus so that nursing students can be as much a part of the activities as the coeds residing there.

A variety of student organizations promote leadership and professionalism, sponsoring activities on state and national levels where nursing students may meet and work with other student nurses and nursing professionals.

Research symposiums, health education programs, continuing education courses, blood pressure screenings, cancer information sessions, and career guidance clinics are offered during the academic year for the public and the health care community.

Financial assistance for students is available through the Office of Financial Aid, Prairie View A&M University, Prairie View, Texas. Nursing scholarships are administered through the Office of the Dean, Houston Clinical Center (797-0722).

SHRINERS HOSPITAL FOR CRIPPLED CHILDREN

1402 Outer Belt Dr. (77030)
713/797-1616

HOURS
Admissions: M–F, 8 AM–4:30 PM (clinic hours vary)
Visiting: 9 AM–9 PM, daily (minimum age: 12)
PARKING
Beside building, patient drop-off/pick-up at entrance; Garage # 4
RECEPTION
Lobby

PARKING   TUNNELS   SKYWALKS   METRO ROUTES: A   B   C

HERMANN PARK

OUTER BELT DRIVE

SOUTH MAIN

HERMANN GARAGE

FANNIN

ROSS STERLING

G4

BEN TAUB GARAGE

G3

M.D. ANDERSON

BELLOWS

E. CULLEN

POLICE

Shriners Hospital for Crippled Children at the Texas Medical Center is one of nineteen orthopedic facilities and three burn institutions sponsored by the Shrine of North America, a social-fraternal organization with a base in Freemasonry, dedicated to service. Twenty of the hospitals are in the United States, with the remaining two located in Canada and Mexico City.

. Shriners Hospital in Houston is a specialty unit that provides orthopedic care and corrective surgery for all children up to the age of 18 without consideration of race or religion. The only criteria for admission are that the children must have an orthopedic problem that can be materially helped and that their parents or guardian are unable to pay for the required medical treatment without placing severe hardship on the family.

Each child is screened by the medical staff to be certain he or she is able to benefit from treatment. Once admitted, no charges are made to the child or the family by either the hospital or the orthopedic surgeons. No insurance payments are accepted.

Its location in the Medical Center allows close affiliations with the University of Texas Medical School and Baylor College of Medicine, which provide Shriners Hospital with a wealth of talent, research, and expertise in orthopedic pediatrics.

The Houston unit was initially housed inside Hermann Hospital and moved into its present building in 1952. Originally known as Arabia Temple Crippled Children's Clinic, the facility was owned, supported, and operated by Arabia Temple in Houston.

In 1966, the national organization assumed ownership of the hospital, and it became the Houston Unit of Shriners Hospitals for Crippled Children.

Support for the hospital comes from donations and the annual Hospital Benefit Day. Patients come from all parts of Texas and neighboring states. They are often provided transportation to and from Houston by Shriners in their areas.

Shriners Hospital does more than merely treat physical problems. A sincere, loving effort is made to have each child feel at home during his or her stay. The hospital stay is made as unlike a hospital experience as possible. Normal living activities are a part of therapy so that the children can learn to cope with their handicaps.

In addition to rooms for boys and girls, the building provides administrative offices, modern diagnostic facilities, an up-to-date operating suite, a recovery room, and areas for physical and occupational therapy. A complete gym and hydrogymnasium (a heated swimming pool of varying depths) offer rehabilitative training. Recent renovations have improved the building's appearance as well as patient flow, efficiency, and privacy.

Children continue their schooling as inpatients with a qualified teacher from the Houston Independent School District, who instructs all grade levels. Along with activities and entertainment provided by Shrine-related groups, teachers from the Glassell School give weekly art classes and the Houston Public Library brings movies.

The hospital features its own brace shop, to make and adjust braces as well as customize shoes used in treating certain disorders.

Seventeen outpatient clinics are currently serving thousands of patients and allow families to talk with orthopedic surgeons who specialize in specific fields. Present clinics include cerebral palsy, clubfoot, plaster and special foot, general, hand, leg length discrepancy, Legg-Calvé Perthes, limb deficiency, metabolic, myelodysplasia, neuromuscular, screening, hip, special back, scoliosis, hemi-melia, and osteogenesis imperfecta.

Research programs, begun several years ago, include the gait analysis laboratory, which uses electronic aids to study muscle activities, and a project being carried out in connection with the University of Texas Health Science Center genetics laboratory to identify genetic syndromes, so as to better understand the outcome of proposed treatments.

Typical of the medical profession's devotion to the Houston Unit of Shriners Hospital is the weekly presentation of the most difficult cases to the full staff of orthopedic surgeons and residents. Operations, X rays, and treatments are reviewed so that patients receive full benefit of the surgeons' combined experience and knowledge.

Recent major accomplishments, including clinical advances in the area of pediatric micro-vascular surgery and a unique Child Life Program featuring social integration of the handicapped child into society, clearly show this institution's position of leadership and constant striving for excellence.

More than ten thousand children have been treated as patients and offered the opportunity to live better, more productive lives. It is an enviable record.

The wholly charitable Shriners Hospital currently maintains about forty inpatient beds, providing a home away from home and sympathetic, understanding care for children afflicted from birth or through illness in later life. Donations are appreciated and donor information can be had by calling the main number.

VOLUNTEERS
An energetic group of volunteers provides invalu-able service to Shriners Hospital, assisting in the clinics, transporting patients to and from airports, leading tours, and helping in physical therapy, occupational therapy, and clerical tasks. Call the main number for specific information.

GENERAL INFORMATION
It is a special concern that visitors not come if they have a fever, cold, sore throat, ear infection, or rash or if they have been exposed to a contagious disease, especially chicken pox. This is to prevent patients from contracting illness during periods when they are in susceptible conditions.

Since no charges are made by Shriners Hospital or the medical staff, no financial assistance is needed for medical care. A social worker is available to help arrange transportation of children to and from local airports, referral to community agencies, and other services. Call the main number.

Every other month, a special clinic is held in Harlingen, Texas. This out-reach program is staffed by orthopedic surgeons and allied health professionals or therapists. They travel to the Rio Grande Valley to help cure and control numerous childhood orthopedic diseases still prevalent in that area and in northern Mexico. The team sees one hundred to two hundred patients each clinic day.

6301 Almeda Rd. (77021)
713/748-5021

HOURS
Visiting: 9 AM–8 PM daily (under 12 must be
accompanied by adult)
PARKING
Across from main entrance (requires 4
quarters—change available at front desk)
RECEPTION
Lobby

St. Anthony Center, a nonprofit, long-term nursing
care and rehabilitation facility,is the largest provider of rehabilitation services for the elderly in
Texas. Owned and operated by the Sisters of
Charity of the Incarnate Word, Houston, the center
is a member of the Sisters of Charity Health Care
System, tenth-largest provider of health care in
the United States.

In 1866, Bishop Claude Marie Dubuis, second
bishop of Galveston, asked the Incarnate Word
and Blessed Sacrament Sisters, an order in Lyons,
France, to help establish a hospital in Galveston to
treat victims of yellow fever, diphtheria, and ty-
phoid. Within months, three young sisters opened
a thirty-bed charity hospital in Galveston. It is, today, the oldest private facility in the state.

In 1899, a grateful patient donated forty acres
with a cottage in Houston to the missionary sisters. The following year, a two-story building was
added and was called St. Anthony's Home for the
Aged. In 1966, the present ten-story, 372-bed facility was opened on the same site.

The center is dedicated to total patient care
through a team approach. It is committed to
providing patients and their families a warm,
loving environment that fulfills physical, emotional, spiritual, and social needs. It seeks to give
a feeling of friendship through openness, understanding, and respect. Although St. Anthony Center is a Catholic, Christian institution, patients
come from every religious and ethnic background.

Patients range from 2 to 102 years of age.
There are nearly twelve hundred nursing home
residents and more than two hundred in- and
out-patients. Facilities include a licensed 47-bed
hospital and a 110-bed skilled nursing care and rehabilitation unit. Application for admission is made
upon a doctor's recommendation.

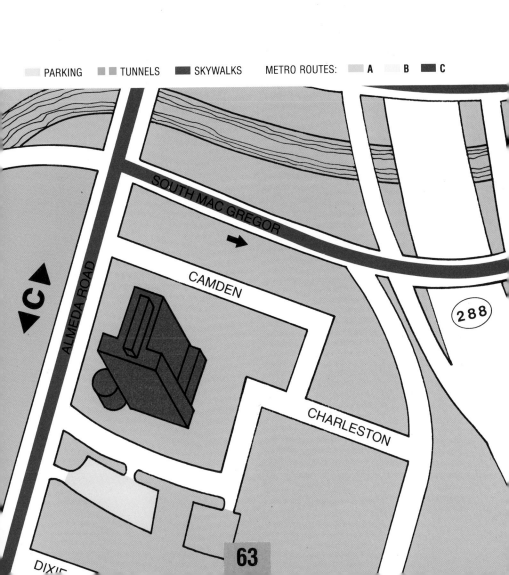

PARKING   TUNNELS   SKYWALKS   METRO ROUTES: A   B   C

SOUTH MAC GREGOR

ALMEDA ROAD

CAMDEN

◀C▶

288

CHARLESTON

DIXIE

The center has the largest amputee clinic in Houston. Amputees, mainly from disease and accidents, undergo therapy and counseling and are fitted with prostheses.

The center offers complete rehabilitative services for many conditions, providing physical and occupational therapy, respiratory therapy, and treatment in speech pathology.

St. Anthony Center became a member of the Texas Medical Center in 1985, but it has had long association with other Medical Center institutions. In 1963, Baylor College of Medicine included St. Anthony patients as a control group in a geriatric neurological study. The University of Texas Health Science Center and UT's M. D. Anderson Hospital and Tumor Institute have been affiliated with St. Anthony Center since the late sixties. Texas Woman's University nursing and allied health students have also received clinical training at the center for many years. Instruction is offered for students of Houston Community College's Health Careers Education Division, as well as those from other area schools.

FOOD SERVICE
The Hogan Dining Room on the first floor offers lunch and dinner. Open 11:30 AM to 12:30 PM, 5:30 PM to 6:30 PM daily. Friends and family may purchase meal tickets from the receptionist or the Business Office to join patients for meals. A cafeteria serves hot lunches Monday through Thursday, from 11:00 AM to 12:30 PM, and a snack bar has sandwiches. Sandwiches are also available in the gift shop.

SHOPPING FACILITIES
A gift shop in the lobby, staffed by volunteers of the Ladies Auxiliary, has gifts, artificial flower arrangements, cards, sundries, stamps, snacks, candy, and fresh sandwiches. It is open every day from 10:00 AM to 3:00 PM.

LIBRARY FACILITIES
Magazines, books (regular and big print), and talking book machines for the blind or visually handicapped are provided for patients by St. Anthony's Volunteer Department.

RELIGIOUS SERVICES
St. Anthony's staff includes a Catholic priest and a Protestant chaplain. The chapel, located on the first floor, is open for meditation daily from about 5:30 AM to about 5:30 PM. Regular religious services are held at the center, and Communion and room visits are an essential function of the Pastoral Care Department.

GUIDED TOURS
Tours can be provided for prospective patients and their families.

VOLUNTEERS
St. Anthony Center has two volunteer groups. The center's program supplies workers for the library, information desk, some offices, and direct patient care. The Ladies Auxiliary provides volunteers for the gift shop, has a group that sews items for the shop, and boasts talented performers, the St. Anthony Singers.

GENERAL INFORMATION
Beauty and barber shop services can be arranged through ward clerks on each floor. Self-service laundry facilities are located on the ground floor. The center's Strake Auditorium is available for activities and performances. Notary public services can be provided upon request.

The Social Service Department helps patients and their families adjust to the center, is especially active in discharge planning, coordinates arrangements for continuing care, and gives information, support, assistance, and counseling whenever needed.

In addition to its complete rehabilitation services, St. Anthony Center offers recreational therapy; crafts, art, and music therapy; and a variety of patient activities, such as entertainment by outside performers, monthly birthday parties for permanent residents, bingo, and so forth.

St. Anthony Center does not receive money from church or tax revenues. It is supported primarily through patient revenue and tax-deductible donations. It is certified for participation in the Medicare and Medicaid programs.

ST. LUKE'S EPISCOPAL HOSPITAL

6720 Bertner Ave. (77030)
713/791-2011
Security: 791-4243

HOURS
Visiting: 9 AM–9 PM daily (minimum age: 10)
Emergency: 24 hours daily (791-2121)
PARKING
Garage #1; Garage #2; limited meters at
entrance (quarters only)
RECEPTION
First floor lobby

PARKING   TUNNELS   SKYWALKS   METRO ROUTES: A   B   C

In the late 1940s, Bishop Clinton S. Quin and the Episcopal Diocese of Texas began planning for the first general hospital to be built in Houston since 1927. The city, which had grown rapidly in population during World War II, was desperately in need of additional hospital services, and the proposal for St. Luke's met with great acceptance.

Opening in 1954, the new, not-for-profit facility was immediately acclaimed as a significant contribution to Houston's medical capabilities. This 931-bed, adult, acute care, teaching, and research institution is directed by a twenty-two–member board. It operates separately from two other organizations (Texas Children's Hospital and Texas Heart Institute), but several departmental or service functions that overlap are shared by these facilities.

Annually, St. Luke's treats almost thirty thousand patients from all parts of the United States and other countries. Over a thousand medical professionals perform more than two million patient-related services. Its medical specialties include cardiology, gastroenterology, obstetrics and gynecology, neurology, nuclear medicine, nutrition, physical medicine, pulmonary disease, radiology, and renal dialysis. The hospital is one of the world's ten major surgical centers. Outstanding surgical fields are ear, nose, and throat; hand; heart; neurosurgery; plastic; orthopedic; spinal; and urological surgeries.

St. Luke's maternity service is family centered and offers parent education classes, has a birthing room, and allows rooming-in. Its High-Risk Obstetrical Program, in conjunction with Texas Children's Hospital and Baylor College of Medicine, has provided a comprehensive diagnosis and treatment for high-risk mothers and their infants.

St. Luke's is one of the institutions affiliated with Baylor College of Medicine. Students, residents, and fellows are an integral part of the health care team.

Not content with an outstanding record for patient care and treatment, St. Luke's has moved to the forefront in selected areas of medical research. The Department of Pathology, for example, through its laboratories, announced an innovative means of oxygen transport, which received federal authorization.

Other research efforts are aimed at the prevention, early diagnosis, and improved treatment of disease. St. Luke's is known for its investigations in diagnostic technology, alleviation of chronic intractable pain, methods of locating primary cancer sites, and heart surgery without transfusion.

Recent projects have focused on early detection of diabetes. The Diabetes Research Laboratory is an important component of a federal grant program to develop a Diabetes and Endocrinology Research Center in conjunction with Baylor College of Medicine.

Pulmonary specialists are continuing their efforts in studying how elements in the blood aggregate to block microcirculation, which leads to pulmonary, cerebral, and other tissue dysfunction following surgery, shock, or infection.

Infectious disease investigators are actively examining common factors held by patients who are attacked by drug-resistant organisms. Their next major work will be in the area of infections caused by surgical wounds or catheter-related incidents.

Nephrologists are looking into the prevention, cause, and treatment of renal failure associated with heart and circulatory system disease.

St. Luke's has been, since its inception, distinguished in each of its fields of endeavor. The hospital's recent link with American Medical International is intended to lower health care costs while maintaining quality and service.

Recent construction at St. Luke's has added four floors with a 57-bed intensive care unit above Texas Heart Institute. A helistop is situated atop the seventh floor. Other additions include three labor/delivery/recovery rooms and two nurseries. As part of a satellite surgery/ambulatory center within St.Luke's, there will be more operating rooms and pre-op areas. A catheterization lab and ultrasound examination rooms are part of the expansion.

FOOD SERVICE

A cafeteria located on the lower level is open 6:30 AM to 10 AM, 11 AM to 4 PM, and 4:45 PM to 8 PM, daily. Visitors are requested to use the facility when it is least crowded—before 10 AM and after 1 PM. A canteen on the second floor of St. Luke's is open 6 AM to 12 PM for snacks and drinks.

SHOPPING FACILITIES

St. Luke's has a gift shop on the first floor by the Texas Heart Institute / Bates Street (heart sculpture) entrance in the main lobby. Grooming aids, a good selection of reading materials, gift items, cards, flowers, candy, and so on may be purchased. Open 8:30 AM to 8:30 PM, daily.

LIBRARY FACILITIES

There is a Medical Staff Library on St. Luke's first floor, which is for the use of staff and students only.

RELIGIOUS SERVICES

A staff of twelve chaplains and nine intern chaplains, representing many denominations, make up the core of St. Luke's Pastoral Care Department. The chaplains visit patients' rooms and administer bedside Communion if desired. Regularly scheduled Christian services are carried on hospital television, as is a Jewish Sabbath service each Friday. To contact one of the chaplains, call 791-3258.

The Cullen Memorial Chapel, located at the Bertner Street lobby, is open 24 hours daily for prayer and meditation. Services are scheduled here throughout the week.

OVERNIGHT ACCOMMODATIONS

Patients in private rooms may have a family member stay overnight. Questions concerning overnight accommodations can be answered by Patient Relations at 791-2900.

GUIDED TOURS

Tours are offered to the general public by the St. Luke's Auxiliary. Arrangements may be made by calling 791-2102.

VOLUNTEERS

St. Luke's has an active volunteer program, which is vital to the operation of the hospital. Various jobs are open. Volunteers operate the gift shop, coffee cart, and patient mail; they help with blood drives, work in the emergency room, the diabetes lab, admissions, development, and other departments; many act as guides and interpreters; others serve as receptionists. Members of St. Luke's Auxiliary also publish a newsletter, *Acts and Facts*.

Those interested in the volunteer program must be at least 17 years old. Information is available by calling the auxiliary director's office at 791-2102.

GENERAL INFORMATION

The Physician Referral Service may be reached at 791-2873.

A 24-hour launderette is near the Bates Street entrance. Washing machines are provided for patients' families. Soap powder may be purchased in the nearby St. Luke's gift shop.

A wide variety of social services, such as referrals for those needing financial assistance to existing community resources, are available through St. Luke's Social Services Department at 791-4324. Other social service programs include crisis intervention and counseling on adapting to illness.

A complete pharmacy is available on the lower level near the Tower Yellow Elevators. Open 24 hours daily, it is primarily for the use of patients in the hospital but serves outpatients as well.

Directories are displayed in the following locations:

1. Texas Heart lobby at the Bates Street entrance. The heart sculpture *Symbol of Excellence* is located at this entrance. The Emergency Center Entrance is on the lower-level drive-through.

2. St. Luke's lobby at the Bertner Street entrance. This entrance faces M. D. Anderson Hospital and Tumor Institute.

3. Texas Children's lobby at the Fannin Street entrance.

To reach a department not located on street level, it is important to use the correct elevator. Each elevator has a different color: Children's Red Elevators, St. Luke's Blue Elevators, Tower Yellow Elevators, St. Luke's Purple Elevators, and Children's Orange Elevators.

CHECK-IN/CHECK-OUT

In order to fill out insurance and financial records, it is helpful for you to have the following:

Medicare/Medicaid I.D. card
Blue Cross or other insurance I.D. card
Military I.D. card if in the U.S. Armed Forces
Social Security number
Driver's license

TEXAS CHILDREN'S HOSPITAL

6621 Fannin St. (77030)
713/791-2831
Security: 791-4243

HOURS
Visiting: 9 AM–9 PM, daily;
Emergency: 24 hours daily (791-2222)
PARKING
Garage #1; Garage#2
RECEPTION
First floor lobby

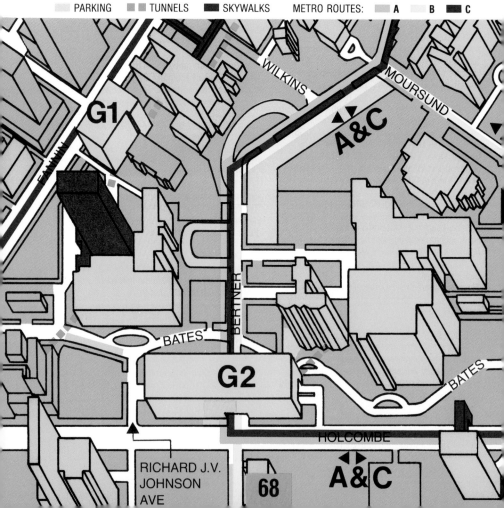

In 1954, the decision was made to design a facility specifically to provide state-of-the-art care for children from birth through adolescence. Based on the concept that the younger patient has special needs and is not just a "little adult," members of the Houston Pediatric Society, the Texas Children's Foundation, and other influential private citizens banded together to form a group to develop the new facility. Until 1954, when Texas Children's admitted its first patients, the majority of seriously ill youngsters in Houston had been treated in their homes. Since those earliest admissions, the hospital has grown to 328 beds and over 12,000 medical staff members. More than 100,000 children are treated annually in thirty-three specialized clinics.

Charged with providing specialized medical care for the diagnosis and treatment of illness in infants, children, and adolescents, the nonprofit organization performs primary as well as secondary diagnosis and follow-up. The staff is dedicated to the special techniques and concerns involved in treating children.

Patient rooms are finished in bright, cheery colors. Parents are encouraged to stay overnight with their children, to provide security and make the hospital stay easier.

The Child Life Program, designed to keep busy young minds active, offers both playroom and bedside attention to support healthy growth during the youngster's stay. Child Life therapists are an integral part of the health care team, working with physicians, nurses, and physical therapists to make a youngster's stay as short and enjoyable as possible. Texas Children's has recently opened an adolescent unit where teenagers can socialize and do school work.

Affiliated with Baylor College of Medicine, Texas Children's provides inpatient and outpatient care. The Emergency Center is staffed twenty-four hours a day to treat patients when immediate medical attention is required.

The Junior League Outpatient Department has thirty-three clinics that deal with the most complex diseases or conditions. All are staffed by pediatricians who are medical and surgical specialists.

The importance of Texas Children's position in the Houston area is seen by the fact that the facility has about 30 percent of all pediatric beds and accounts for around 30 percent of all pediatric discharges.

Both neonatal and pediatric intensive care units are available, staffed with personnel specially trained to respond in crisis situations where only minutes or seconds are left to stabilize a child's condition. The focus of St. Luke's Hospital on high-risk obstetrics is coupled with the availability of Texas Children's intensive care units, so that dangers to newborns are minimized.

Of the thousands of inpatient and day surgical procedures performed annually, many involve highly specialized techniques to correct congenital or acquired abnormalities. A superior nursing staff and consultation with subspecialists ensure that each surgical case will be handled professionally and that each patient is treated with tenderness and love.

Research is an active function of the organization. The Children's Nutrition Research Center has federally funded studies on the nutritional needs of infants and their mothers. In one program, fortified human milk and commercial formulas are being compared to learn which offers the greatest benefit to premature infants. A new eleven-story Nutrition Research Center tower (completion planned for 1987) is one of five human nutrition centers established by the Department of Agriculture and will be operated by Baylor College of Medicine in cooperation with Texas Children's Hospital.

In addition to patient care and research, education plays a powerful role in Texas Children's overall mission. Medical students, residents, and fellows are all provided with the experience of dealing with child patients and are able to learn from the excellent staff.

FOOD SERVICE
A cafeteria located on the lower level is open 6:30 AM to 10 AM, 11 AM to 4 PM, and 4:45 PM to 8 PM, daily. Visitors are requested to use the facility when it is least crowded—before 10 AM and after 1 PM. A coffee shop on the first floor by the Orange Elevators is open Monday through Friday, 7 AM to 3 AM; and Saturday and Sunday, 8:30 AM to 3 AM.

SHOPPING FACILITIES
Texas Children's has a toy store off the Fannin Street lobby on the first floor. This shop is specifically oriented toward children, with dolls, stuffed animals, books, games, and toys. Open 8:30 AM to 8 PM, Monday through Friday; 9:30 AM to 5 PM, Saturday and Sunday.

LIBRARY FACILITIES
The Parent Resource Room and Children's Library on the fifth floor was initially funded by Pi Beta Phi Sorority. The library is an extension of the Child Life/Play Therapy Department, whose purpose is to provide for the social, developmental, and emotional needs of hospitalized children. There also is a Medical Staff Library on the first floor for the use of staff and students only.

RELIGIOUS SERVICES

A staff of chaplains, representing many denominations, visit patients' rooms and administer bedside Communion if desired. Regularly scheduled Christian services are carried on hospital television, as is a Jewish Sabbath service each Friday. To contact one of the chaplains, call 791-3258.

The Cullen Memorial Chapel, located at the Bertner Street lobby, is open 24 hours daily for prayer and meditation. Services are scheduled here throughout the week.

OVERNIGHT ACCOMMODATIONS

Parents of children in Texas Children's are encouraged to stay overnight. Questions concerning overnight accommodations can be answered by Patient Relations at 791-3025.

GUIDED TOURS

Tours are offered to patients and their families by the Auxiliary to Texas Children's Hospital. Arrangements can be made by calling 791-2255.

Medical students and allied health students are invited to attend tours, which are scheduled on a regular basis. Tours need to be set up one week in advance.

VOLUNTEERS

Texas Children's has an active volunteer program vital to the operation of the hospital. Many jobs are open. Volunteers are hostesses, guides, interpreters, office clerical workers, receptionists, patient pals, and assistant aids to professionals. There are openings for volunteers in the toy shop, coffee shop, and many departments. Members of Texas Children's Auxiliary also publish *Watch* magazine. Those interested in the volunteer program must be at least fourteen years old. Information is available by calling the auxiliary director's office at 791-2255.

The Junior League of Houston supports the Junior League Outpatient Department. League volunteers serve in several other areas of Texas Children's and are active in the Child Life/Play Therapy program.

GENERAL INFORMATION

Texas Children's has several extras for patients and their guests. There are playrooms for creative fun and learning. A TV rental service is offered, and a volunteer bookmobile brings a large selection of children's books.

A teen room has electronic games, a pinball machine, piano, jukebox, pool table, and many games. It is open to patients twelve years of age and older (no parents allowed) who have a hospital identification bracelet. Each may bring one adolescent guest.

A 24-hour launderette is near the Bates Street entrance. Washing machines are provided for patients' families. Soap powder may be purchased in the nearby gift shop.

Texas Children's Physician Referral Service may be reached at 791-4357. For youngsters who need home health care, Texas Children's has a program that includes home visits by nurses, aides, therapists, nutritionists, and social workers.

A wide variety of social services is available through the Social Services Department at 791-2149. Programs include crisis intervention and counseling on adapting to illness, as well as referrals to existing community resources. The Junior League Clinic Service helps certain patients with complex medical needs.

A complete pharmacy is available on the lower level near the Tower Yellow Elevators. Open 24 hours daily, it is primarily for the use of patients in the hospital but serves outpatients as well.

Questions focusing on arrangements and accommodations in the hospital for visitors and families are usually answered by auxiliary volunteers, who staff the reception and information desks. For information about outpatient care, telephone the clinic at 791-3291.

To reach a department not located on street level, it is important to use the correct elevator. Each elevator has a different color: Children's Red Elevators, St. Luke's Blue Elevators, Tower Yellow Elevators, St. Luke's Purple Elevators, and Children's Orange Elevators.

Each Spring, Texas Children's and St. Luke's hold a neonatal reunion to celebrate the growth of infants born prematurely and others who spent a length of time in the neonatal intensive and intermediate care units or the premature nursery. The party, in a big tent at Texas Children's parking lot, brings together growing "graduates" and their parents with the hospital and medical personnel who spent so much time with them.

TEXAS HEART INSTITUTE

1101 Bates St. (77030)
713/791-4011
Security: 791–4243

HOURS
Visiting: 9 AM–9 PM, daily (minimum age: 10)
Emergency: 24 hours daily
PARKING
Garage #1; Garage #2
RECEPTION
First floor lobby

By 1962, both St. Luke's Episcopal Hospital and Texas Children's Hospital were deeply involved in cardiovascular medicine. Directors and trustees recognized the necessity for an institution dedicated to the heart and the circulatory system. The creation of Texas Heart Institute fulfilled the need for education, research, and medical/surgical treatment of cardiovascular and related diseases in adults and children.

Charged to oversee the care of St. Luke's and Texas Children's patients, it is, today, the only Texas Medical Center facility devoted totally to specialties of the heart and the blood vessels.

Texas Heart is not a hospital. It is, rather, an institutional program of education, treatment, and research of cardiovascular diseases. Since its opening, over sixty thousand open heart procedures have been performed at the institute, including the first U.S. heart transplant. An average of twenty-five to thirty heart operations are performed each day.

This not-for-profit organization has become a major international referral center for cardiovascular care. Of the nearly 6,000 adult and pediatric patients who received cardiovascular surgery in a recent fiscal year, 33 percent came from foreign countries and 38 percent from outside the general Houston area. Additionally, 5,455 heart patients were treated nonsurgically in the same year, with 19 percent coming from outside the United States.

Working with the staff of Texas Children's, the institute is now recognized as one of the world's leading centers for treatment of children with heart conditions. Exceptional cases are regularly referred from other hospitals throughout the world.

True to the original founding concept of placing a high value on education, training programs are held for physicians, nurses, and other personnel. In keeping with the theme of innovation, special classes were held on the use of streptokinase as a treatment in heart attack situations. This drug, administered properly, shows promising results in preserving heart muscle tissue that might otherwise be damaged.

The institute's educational programs have trained cardiologists, cardiovascular surgeons and nurses, anesthesiologists, and cardiac catheterization and perfusion technologists. Hundreds of dedicated, motivated individuals completed their schooling under the institute's teaching staff and faculty from and UT Medical School through the renowned residency and fellowship programs, while additional professionals have graduated in allied health fields.

The unique Biocommunications Laboratory, which provides videotapes of heart sounds and shows the heart in matching action, has produced a series of tapes for use in self- and classroom teaching.

Clinical and basic studies have led to the development of equipment and techniques now used by heart specialists worldwide. Research, a never-ending task, was rewarded during the study of the drug papaverine, which was being used to treat patients with coronary vasospasm (unexpected spasm of blood vessels to the heart, causing the heart to fail to contract). Beneficial results have led to a study to see if it might now be administered to a greater number of heart surgery patients.

The Nuclear Medicine Department has continued to improve its techniques for producing images of the heart and has developed a way to consistently measure movement of the heart's walls. This achievement was cited as a significant development in the field at a recent International Meeting of Nuclear Medicine and Biology.

New ways of placing heart pacemakers, especially in children, also came from an institute project, which promises to bring pacemaker technology to many heretofore impossible-to-fit patients.

Other research activities include refinements in a type of implanted heart assist device, artificial heart systems, use of lasers to remove blockage in coronary arteries, and computer analysis of individuals with severe cardiac arrhythmia. Research efforts have produced such accomplishments as grafts and valves that improve blood flow and a balloon pump that circulates blood freely during surgery.

A major facility expansion provides a significant

increase in the number of intensive care beds, as well as added space for education, surgical support, and diagnostic services.

Dr. Denton A. Cooley, founder of Texas Heart Institute, is a pioneer in heart surgery. He performed the nation's first human heart transplant in 1968 and implanted the first totally artificial heart in a human in 1969. He has completed well over fifty thousand open-heart operations. The Houston heart surgeon was awarded the Medal of Freedom, the nation's highest civilian award, in 1984 by President Ronald Reagan.

FOOD SERVICE
A cafeteria located on the lower level is open 6:30 AM to 10 AM, 11 AM to 4 PM, and 4:45 PM to 8 PM, daily. Visitors are requested to use the facility when it is least crowded—before 10 AM and after 1 PM. A canteen on the second floor is open 6 AM to 12 PM for snacks and drinks.

RELIGIOUS SERVICES
A staff of twelve chaplains and nine intern chaplains, representing many denominations, make up the core of St. Luke's Pastoral Care Department. The chaplains visit patients' rooms and administer bedside Communion if desired. Regularly scheduled Christian services are carried on hospital television, as is a Jewish Sabbath service each Friday. To contact one of the chaplains, call 791-3258.

The Cullen Memorial Chapel, located at the Bertner Street lobby, is open 24 hours daily for prayer and meditation. Services are scheduled here throughout the week.

OVERNIGHT ACCOMMODATIONS
Patients in private rooms may have a family member stay overnight. Parents of children are encouraged to spend the night. Questions concerning overnight accommodations can be answered by Patient Relations at 791-2900.

GUIDED TOURS
Tours are offered to the public by St. Luke's auxiliary. Arrangements can be made by calling 791-2102.

VOLUNTEERS
Texas Heart Institute is served by the auxiliaries of St. Luke's Episcopal Hospital and Texas Children's Hospital.

GENERAL INFORMATION
There is a 24-hour launderette near the Texas Heart / Bates Street entrance. Washing machines are provided for patients' families. Soap powder may be purchased in the nearby St. Luke's gift shop.

A complete pharmacy is available on the lower level near the Tower Yellow Elevators. Open 24 hours daily, it is primarily for the use of patients in the hospital but serves outpatients as well.

Questions focusing on arrangements and accommodations in the hospital for visitors and families are usually answered by auxiliary volunteers, who staff the reception and information desks.

Directories are displayed in the following locations:

1. Texas Heart lobby at the Bates Street entrance. The heart sculpture *Symbol of Excellence* is located at this entrance. The Emergency Center Entrance is on the lower-level drive-through.

2. St. Luke's lobby at the Bertner Street entrance. This entrance faces M. D. Anderson Hospital and Tumor Institute.

3. Texas Children's lobby at the Fannin Street entrance.

To reach a department not located on street level, it is important to use the correct elevator. Each elevator has a different color: Children's Red Elevators, St. Luke's Blue Elevators, Tower Yellow Elevators, St. Luke's Purple Elevators, and Children's Orange Elevators.

Symbol of Excellence, the sculpture outside Texas Heart Institute (Bates Street) Entrance, was created by Theodore H. (Ted) McKinney (1918–1983). Mr. McKinney, a native of Bethel, Vermont, became interested in abstract forms and started sculpting with driftwood as a young man in the U.S. Navy. After retiring from a successful business career in 1975, he was able to devote more attention to his art.

Mr. McKinney was a friend and former patient of Dr. Denton Cooley, who admired several of his works. Dr. Cooley commissioned him to sculpt a heart-shaped figure. Mr. McKinney designed the piece as an expression of gratitude for heart surgery performed on his daughter, and later himself, at the institute.

The heart is made of red granite quarried in Cold Springs, Minnesota, and the black granite base came from California. The sculpture stands seven feet tall and weighs 6,700 pounds. *Symbol of Excellence,* dedicated in 1977, is a lasting tribute to the accomplishments and goals of Texas Heart Institute.

1130 M. D. Anderson Blvd. (77030)
713/794-2000
Security: 794-2222 or 794-2158

HOURS
M–F, 7 AM–6 PM
PARKING
Limited meters by dormitories (quarters only);
surface lot across street; Garage #1; Garage
#3
RECEPTION
Lobbies of Mary Gibbs Jones Hall, Education
Building, and South and North residences

PARKING ■ ■ TUNNELS ■ ■ SKYWALKS METRO ROUTES: ■ ■ **A** ■ **B** ■ **C**

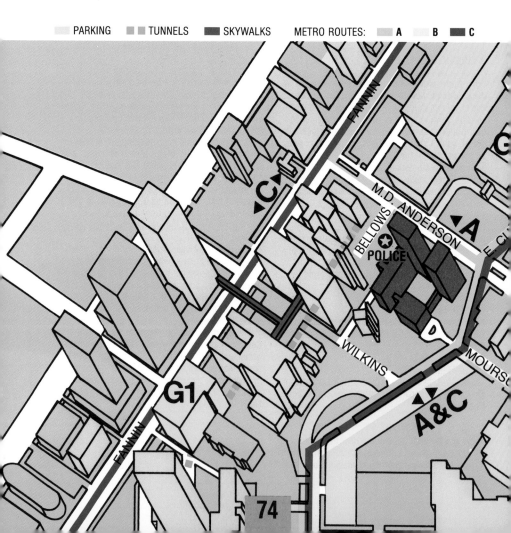

Texas Woman's University, the largest women's university in the United States, is a state-supported multipurpose school, founded in 1901 by the Texas Legislature. Its main campus is located in Denton. There are three additional centers for upper-level and graduate-level instruction in health sciences, two in Dallas and one in the Texas Medical Center. Although the school has traditionally been exclusively for women, men are eligible for admission in graduate and health science studies.

The Houston campus of TWU, established in 1960, was begun as a center for clinical instruction in nursing for upper-level undergraduates. By 1962, occupational and physical therapy were added to the curriculum. TWU now offers many different programs in seven health care disciplines. Besides nursing, occupational therapy, and physical therapy, courses include health care administration, nutrition and food sciences, biology, and counseling psychology. Nursing and occupational and physical therapy are presented for undergraduates and graduates; the remaining are graduate-level programs. Bachelors', masters', and doctors' degrees are conferred by the university.

The TWU complex consists of four buildings: North and South Residence halls, the Education Building, and Mary Gibbs Jones Hall, which houses administrative and faculty offices, classrooms, and laboratories. The facilities were built with a mixture of private and federal funds. As a young congressman, George Bush encouraged then President Lyndon Johnson to lift a moratorium on federal funds to allow construction of this facility.

Enrollment at both undergraduate and graduate levels has increased each semester. Recently, over twelve hundred students registered for classes, more than eight hundred at the graduate level.

The TWU's Houston Center maintains the most advanced educational resources, which include research labs in biochemistry, nutrition, occupational and physical therapy, and anatomy. Electromyographic (EMG), biofeedback, and bone densitometry equipment are used regularly in instruction.

More housing is provided by TWU Houston than any other school on the Medical Center grounds. It has resident accommodations for over five hundred, supplying space for TWU students and other institutions.

The university has the only scholastic programs in the Medical Center in such areas as occupational and physical therapy and health care administration.

TWU is linked to the other Medical Center institutions because of its central location and continuing education programs, which offer health professionals at Medical Center hospitals advanced degree work in many disciplines. The opportunity for further schooling at TWU has given advantages to neighboring institutions in terms of employee recruitment and retention. Staff members who have participated in TWU programs have stayed longer at their respective institutions, have realized improved chances of career advancement, and have found expanded routes for professional growth.

TWU Houston is recognized for its health professional undergraduate- and graduate-level education. It offers masters' programs in nutrition and counseling psychology. It is the only Houston-area institution with a Ph.D. program in nursing. The doctoral program in nursing admitted its first students in 1983. TWU Houston is the only school in the central United States offering a Ph.D. degree in physical therapy. This program is the first in the United States at a state-supported institution of higher education.

TWU's preeminent Houston Center provides an outstanding number of programs in nursing and allied health education through its unique facilities. Courses are open to entry-level and advanced pupils. Consistent growth is expected to continue with the addition of new graduate programs in nursing and allied health.

The school is particularly sensitive to the requirements of mature, returning students. Flexible schedules are available, with courses being given in the evenings and on weekends. The school encourages and supports practicing nurses and other professional men and women in undergraduate, graduate, and continuing education.

FOOD SERVICE
TWU's cafeteria, located in the basement of the South Residence Hall, serves breakfast and lunch, 6:30 AM to 2:00 PM, and light dinners, 4:30 PM to 8:00 PM, Monday through Friday.

SHOPPING FACILITIES
A bookstore is located on the first floor, southwest corner, of the South Residence Hall. It is open Monday through Friday, 9:30 AM to 5:30 PM. The TWU bookstore has school supplies, magazines, texts and references, paperbacks, T-shirts, gift items, and convenience-store food.

LIBRARY FACILITIES
Students and faculty use the Houston Academy of Medicine–Texas Medical Center Library. There is also a Learning Resource Center on the second floor of Mary Gibbs Jones Hall, where students have access to audiovisual materials.

OVERNIGHT ACCOMMODATIONS
Overnight accommodations are offered to visiting scholars and guests of TWU-Houston Center in the two residence halls, which primarily house students.

GUIDED TOURS
Tours are arranged upon request; contact campus administration.

GENERAL INFORMATION
Faculty, staff, and students have a lounge on the second floor of Mary Gibbs Jones Hall. The South Residence Hall has a commuting students lounge on the first floor. A student recreation room is also located on the first floor of the South Residence Hall. An exercise room in the basement of the North Residence Hall is available for faculty, staff, and students.

The Student Affairs Office arranges events and excursions for students. Classic movies, groups, bands, and speakers are brought to the campus. Outings range from weekly van trips to the grocery store to visits to ethnic restaurants, concerts, cultural events, area festivals, and tours to Galveston.

A variety of social services are available for students. A counseling center is located in Mary Gibbs Jones Hall on the sixth floor. Professional senior staff counselors provide information and guidance, including a wide variety of self-improvement programs. A student development coordinator's office is located on the first floor of the North Residence Hall.

A full range of financial assistance is offered to students through the Office of Financial Aids in Mary Gibbs Jones Hall (room 924).

Special help programs are available for students. These include computer services, which are available through the Computer Center on the tenth floor of Mary Gibbs Jones Hall, and tutoring services, which may be arranged through the Office of Personnel Services on the ninth floor.

UNIVERSITY OF HOUSTON COLLEGE OF PHARMACY

1441 Moursund Ave. (77030)
713/796-8297

HOURS
M–F, 9 AM–5 PM
PARKING
Garage #5; Garage #6; limited meters
beside building (quarters only)
RECEPTION
Lobby

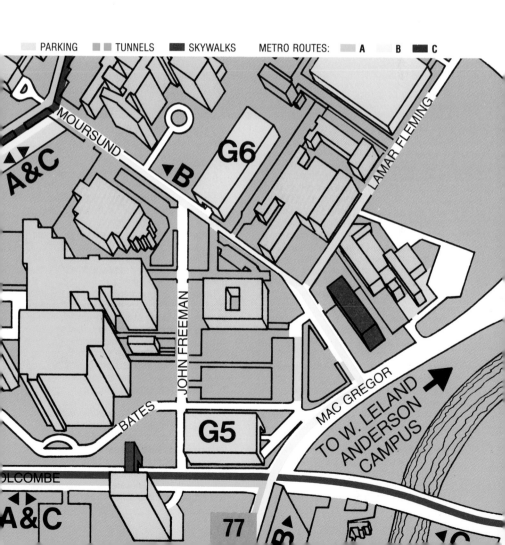

The University of Houston's nationally recognized College of Pharmacy was established in 1947 and began operation in the Texas Medical Center in 1980. Departments that require a patient population, including pharmaceutics, clinical pharmacy, and part of the pharmacology program, are housed in a five-story building on land donated by the Medical Center. The rest of the department of pharmacology, along with the department of medicinal chemistry and pharmacognosy, remains on the main University of Houston campus.

The college educates and trains students to become practitioners of pharmacy; offers graduate programs for researchers in pharmacology, pharmaceutics, medicinal chemistry, and hospital pharmacy administration; provides drug information to professionals and the public through the Turner Drug Information Center; and conducts research in pharmacology, medicinal chemistry, pharmacokinetics (kinetic behavior of drugs), pharmacognosy (physical characteristics of crude drugs), clinical pharmacy, and hospital pharmacy. The facility has no provisions for patient care and does not operate a dispensing pharmacy.

The college offers a three-year professional program leading to a bachelor of science degree. It is open to students who have completed a two-year prepharmacy program or its equivalent. Of particular interest is a clinical clerkship at hospitals in the Medical Center and an externship rotation through hospitals, clinics, and community pharmacies.

A program leading to an M.S. in Hospital Pharmacy provides advanced training for director of pharmacy services positions. A B.S. in Pharmacy is required for this course, which takes three semesters plus a summer session.

Graduate programs are available for M.S. and Ph.D. degrees in pharmacology. The first year of study includes structured basic courses, but the particular path a degree candidate follows is determined by individual interests.

The Turner Drug Information Center (TDIC), located on the first floor of the College of Pharmacy Building, makes use of computer and microfiche retrieval systems and all current resources to answer questions about drug identification and availability, usage, drug therapy, side effects, toxicity, drug interactions, incompatibilities, alternate treatments, dosages, and research on new drugs. TDIC responds to almost six thousand inquiries a year.

This important service is available without charge to physicians, pharmacists, dentists, veterinarians, and the general public, Monday through Friday, from 9:00 AM to 5:00 PM. Written responses, documentation, and literature citations are available upon request. There is a 24-hour "on call" service for patient-care emergencies. Texas residents outside area code 713 can call TDIC collect at the 796-9297 number.

The Pharmacy Building also houses a sterile products laboratory for research on sterile products and intravenous fluids, a clinical pharmacokinetics lab to determine drug levels in blood and other body fluids, a biopharmaceutics and pharmacology teaching lab, a dispensing pharmacy laboratory, and research laboratories for the departments of pharmaceutics, clinical pharmacy, and pharmacology.

While the college is primarily an educational institution at undergraduate and graduate levels, its professors have made many important contributions through research. Investigations include projects on patient drug therapy; drug absorption, distribution, metabolism, and excretion; prediction of drug behavior; drug interactions; and patient acceptance of new dosage forms. The main thrust is to discover ways to improve administering and monitoring drugs with the optimal level for therapeutic activity and minimal side effects.

The school's renowned Institute for Cardiovascular Studies, which has drawn together interested faculty from several colleges of the University of Houston, is conducting research on various cardiovascular diseases and potential drugs for treatment.

Professors in the department of pharmaceutics are analyzing the effects of drugs in open-heart surgery patients; studying drug treatment for kidney stones; examining drug interactions with anticoagulants; and investigating better ways to prescribe antibiotics for children. They continue to research how drugs and their byproducts are treated by the liver, the body's main drug-eliminating organ.

A clinical pharmacy faculty researcher was able to alleviate the pain of mouth ulcers in cancer-chemotherapy patients with his development of a popsiclelike nystatin, an antibiotic effective in treatment of infections of mucous membranes.

Modern pharmacists are trained to be more than druggists. They must become active members of the health care team and drug information specialists for the medical and allied health professions, as well as health information specialists for their communities. The department of clinical pharmacy and administration appoints faculty to Hermann Hospital, M. D. Anderson Hospital and Tumor Institute, Methodist Hospital, and the Veterans Administration Medical Center to train students in clinical pharmacy. Students are assigned patients and are responsible for recording drug histories, monitoring drug responses, and counseling.

The college is also closely tied to other institutions in the Medical Center through the Houston Pharmacological Center. This consortium is made up of pharmacology departments from the University of Texas Medical School at Houston, Baylor College of Medicine, and University of Houston. A training grant supporting four predoctoral pharmacology students from each school has been funded through 1987.

Electronic technology plays an important role in the modern, patient-oriented profession of pharmacy. University of Houston's researchers have developed computer programs for monitoring and reviewing drug utilization. Mathematical and statistical methods are being used to produce correct dosages of certain drugs.

The college is actively involved with the community. It conducts free hypertension screenings and provides speakers on drug-related topics.

Information concerning scholarships and financial assistance for students is obtained by speaking with the college administrator at 749-4106.

GUIDED TOURS
A tour of the building can be arranged by calling the College of Pharmacy.

THE UNIVERSITY OF TEXAS HEALTH SCIENCE CENTER AT HOUSTON

1100 Holcombe Blvd. (77225)
713/792-2121
Security: 792-2890
Emergency: 792-HELP (4357)

HOURS
M–F, 8 AM–5 PM
PARKING
Visitors announce themselves at gate
RECEPTION
South entrance hall

PARKING · · TUNNELS · · SKYWALKS   METRO ROUTES: A   B   C

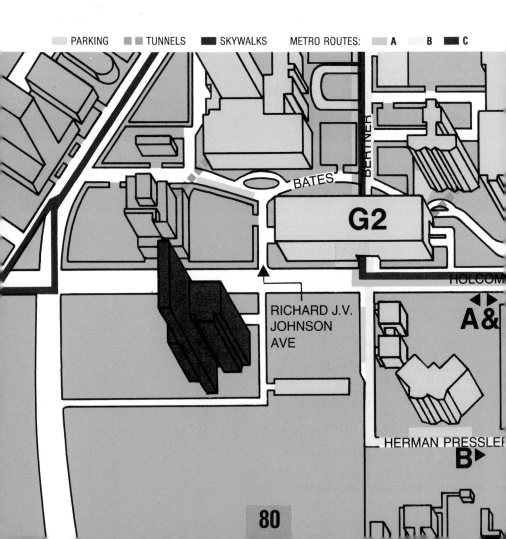

BERTNER

BATES

G2

HOLCOM

RICHARD J.V.
JOHNSON
AVE

A&

HERMAN PRESSLE

B▶

The University of Texas Health Science Center at Houston (UTHSCH) is a health sciences university of the highest caliber. It is recognized by the people of Texas and the United States as a leader in contributing to health education, research, and care through the development of human resources and knowledge and providing exemplary services. While the main effort is educational, emphasis is also placed on research and service programs.

Eight units make up the present UTHSCH group: the Dental Branch, the Division of Continuing Education, the Graduate School of Biomedical Sciences, the Medical School (which includes the Mental Sciences Institute), the School of Allied Health Sciences, the School of Nursing, the School of Public Health, and the Speech and Hearing Institute. Each component will be treated individually; an overview, however, is helpful.

UTHSCH is impossible to define in terms of one professional group or discipline. It reflects the combined efforts of many individuals working together for human well being and scientific progress. Deeply involved in patient care and strongly committed to the curative and preventive roles of medicine, UTHSCH is more than a medical school. Education, its first responsibility, is backed by efforts in the fields of research, communications, humanities, law, and finance.

UTHSCH is the largest of six health-related institutions in the University of Texas System and serves as one of two components in Houston. The UT System Cancer Center/M. D. Anderson Hospital and Tumor Institute is the other (see p. 103). Both institutions share some faculty members and clinical facilities but are operated separately, with individual administrations, budgets, and functions.

In addition to the primary programs in the schools, a number of centers and institutions offer cross-disciplinary studies of more specialized topics, including the Analytical Chemistry Center, the Center for Demographics and Population Genetics, the Center for Health Promotion Research and Development, the Dental Science Institute, the Human Nutrition Center, the Institute for Technology Development and Assessment, the Institute of Environmental Health, the Medical Genetics Center, the Sensory Sciences Center, and the Toxicology Center.

Hermann Hospital serves as the main teaching hospital for UTHSCH, acting as a center for patient care and clinical study for faculty and students. Joint Hermann Hospital–UTHSCH projects include the emergency and trauma center, the organ transplant program, and the Texas Kidney Institute. A network of teaching affiliations with Houston-area hospitals (Memorial Hospital System, St.

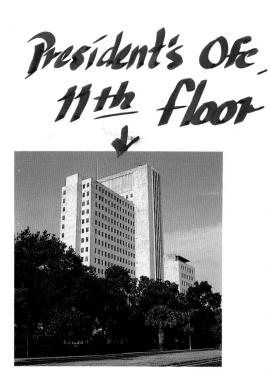

President's Ofc, 11th floor

Joseph Hospital, St. Anthony Center, Texas Heart Institute, and Shriners Hospital) serves an even greater patient population.

Established in 1972, UTHSCH has advanced a tradition of excellence and achievement, while building an academic community devoted to the development of scientific and human potential.

Approximately 1.5 million square feet of space are used by about 700 fulltime faculty members, 2,600 students, and almost 2,500 full- and part-time nonfaculty personnel. Over a quarter million medical and dental patients are cared for in a normal year. Annually, research grants amounting to more than $20 million are awarded to various departments from government and private funds.

The nineteen-story Houston Main Building on Holcombe Boulevard houses administrative offices, human resources and employee relations (personnel), security, the registrar's office, a cafeteria, the Nursing School, student financial aid, accounting, and an outdoor fitness center. The Main Building is still occasionally referred to as the "Prudential Building." It was the Houston home of Prudential Insurance Company until purchased by UTHSCH in 1974. No patients are treated in the Main Building.

UT/TV-Houston, part of the Office of University Relations located in the Houston Main Building, both produces and transmits programming and is working in conjunction with commercial television stations to deliver health programs throughout Texas and in a number of other states. The cable and microwave transmission systems also provide special programming as a service for pediatrics patients throughout the Medical Center and continuing health care education programs for its health facilities, as well as hospitals elsewhere in Houston on a subscription basis.

FOOD SERVICE
A full-service cafeteria on the second floor is open for breakfast and lunch, 7:30 AM to 2:30 PM, Monday through Friday. Machines vending snacks are available on the sixth and seventh floors. A confectionery is on the first floor.

OVERNIGHT ACCOMMODATIONS
There are none in the Houston Main Building.

In 1980, a fund-raising program targeted on the need for a student-faculty housing complex to accommodate visitors, new arrivals, and long-term residents. A $14-million bond issue was sold; and today, between the Medical Center and the Astrodome, situated on University of Texas land, a 500-apartment complex (University Housing, 7900 Cambridge Street), completed in the summer of 1982, serves this need. The project offers con-

venient location, shuttle service to the Medical Center, laundry facilities, and superior security services. A 150-child day care center, open to children of students, faculty, and staff, is located in the complex. For information, call 792-8112.

GENERAL INFORMATION
The Main Building offers an outdoor olympic-size swimming pool (open May through September), tennis courts, jogging track, and picnic areas for the use of faculty, staff, students, and their families. Those connected with UT may join the recreation center on the eighth floor of the UT Medical School. Facilities include basketball, volley ball, and squash/racquetball courts; weight and exercise rooms; a game room; a TV room; and a sauna. A new recreation center adjacent to the UT apartments has tennis, basketball, and racquetball courts; a 50-meter pool; athletic fields; and a clubhouse.

Information concerning financial aid for students (792-4260) is available on the sixth floor of the Main Building. The Student Counseling Service (792-4284) is on the fifth floor. A special employee assistance program, dealing with financial as well as other problems, offers confidential counseling and referral. For information, call 792-4802. Other employee relations matters are administered through the first-floor Human Resources Office (792-4290).

Brown-bag lunchtime programs are offered for UT employees each month on topics as varied as jogging and coping with grief. Special evening seminars are also conducted. Training courses to enhance the individual employee's development are given on a regular basis. Call Human Resources (792-4290) for further information and schedules.

The monumental sculpture at the center of the fountain of UTHSCH Main Building's Holcombe Boulevard entrance represents the American family. *Wave of Life,* carved from a single block of limestone, was created by American sculptor Wheeler Williams for the former Prudential Building. The 1952 Peter Hurd fresco *The Future Belongs to Those Who Prepare for It* is in the Main Building.

THE UNIVERSITY OF TEXAS HEALTH SCIENCE CENTER AT HOUSTON
DENTAL BRANCH

6516 John Freeman Ave. (77030)
713/792-4021
Security: 792-2890
Emergency: 792-HELP (4357)

HOURS
Clinic: M–F, 8 AM–5 PM
PARKING
Garage #6; handicapped drop-off/pick-up at entrance
RECEPTION
First floor lobby

PARKING ■ ■ TUNNELS ■ SKYWALKS METRO ROUTES: ■ A ■ B ■ C

MOURSUND

LAMAR FLEMING

A&C

▼B

G6

JOHN FREEMAN

BATES

G5

HOLCOMBE

A&C

MAC GREGOR

TO W. LELAND ANDERSON CAMPUS

B▼

C

In 1905, the Texas Dental College was founded by a group of Houston professionals and businessmen. Thirty-eight years later, in 1943, the college became the University of Texas School of Dentistry. The school remained in the original Texas Dental College facilities near downtown Houston until completion of its current building in the Texas Medical Center in 1955. It became the Dental Branch when it joined seven other institutions as part of UTHSCH in 1972. The Dental Branch is the oldest unit, since it came under the University of Texas jurisdiction in 1943.

The school offered only doctor of dental surgery (D.D.S.) degrees to its students until 1951, when the postgraduate school was opened. Since then, many programs have been added. The Dental Branch has undergraduate, graduate, and postgraduate courses in dentistry, dental hygiene, and dental assisting; it also has continuing education classes, as well as research activities.

There are four divisions of the Dental Branch: the Postgraduate School, which provides advanced studies for dentists; the School of Dental Hygiene, offering a two-year diploma course; the Dental Assisting Program, a one-year certificate program; and the Dental Science Institute, which conducts dental research.

The Dental Science Institute is housed in the old Texas Dental College building (at Fannin and Blodgett streets) near downtown. The UT Board of Regents has authorized architectural plans to in-

corporate the institute into the Dental Branch building in the Medical Center. Work is underway on a new five-level addition.

The Dental Branch provides trained practitioners through its many educational programs. At this writing, over 600 students are enrolled in the various plans. Each year the school graduates about 120 dentists, 40 dental hygienists, and 10 dental assistants.

A self-directed D.D.S. degree program emphasizes preventive dentistry. The curriculum allows students to pace themselves, progressing at various rates, and has enabled many to graduate early. This innovative course maximizes individual teaching and counseling. Undergraduates are introduced to patient clinical care in their first year. Two-to-four-year graduate and postgraduate courses are offered in seven specialties.

The Dental Branch is dedicated to transmitting new knowledge to the dental health profession through its continuing education courses. These one-to-three-day seminars are given for practicing dentists throughout the year.

Research is designed to increase understanding of causes of dental problems, prevention of disease, and improvement in treatments. An electron microscope and other advanced equipment facilitates the study of dental diseases and their origins.

The Dental Branch offers treatment and preventive instruction to more than ten thousand

Houstonians and reaches out to others in clinics throughout the area and the state. With faculty supervision and assistance, student dentists treat patients as a part of their training. Simple dental cases are preferred by the clinic because they are better suited for learning. The main considerations for patient selection are (a) student requirement needs; (b) ability, skill level, and student's time remaining in school to complete a treatment; and (c) availability of patients to make frequent, and sometimes long, appointments.

Patients who are accepted must have treatment needs that fit into the teaching program. Fees vary; patients are charged only for materials used. Appointment hours are between 8:00 AM and 5:00 PM. To find out if you qualify as a patient, call 792-4056.

Undergraduates also teach proper oral health care to youngsters in the Houston Independent School District and provide indigent dental care at the Laredo–Webb County Health Department in Laredo and at the Goodwill Clinic in Houston. They treat physically and mentally handicapped patients at the Dental Branch and the Goodwill Clinic. Dental faculty and students staff a pedodontic clinic in Texas Children's Hospital. As a clinical teaching institution, the Dental Branch makes high-quality dental care available at minimal cost.

The school provides treatment and disease prevention to hospitalized patients as well as outpatients. Besides observing surgical operations and hospital procedures, undergraduates participate in dental and oral operations. There is a particular interest in treating trauma victims.

Staff and students have pioneered in many new fields. Recent work has been in implementation of the "lingual" (invisible) orthodontic technique; the use of dental laminates (bonding); ceramics (for crowns) first developed for nose cones in guided missiles; pit and fissure sealants; denture implants; and orthognathic surgery procedures. The school also has been actively involved in a gerontology program.

FOOD SERVICE
A cafeteria/snack bar on the second floor serves beverages, snacks, sandwiches, and lunches from 7:30 AM to 1:30 PM on weekdays.

SHOPPING FACILITIES
A bookstore is for students only.

LIBRARY FACILITIES
A library with medical and dental literature and special audiovisual equipment is available for faculty and student use.

1100 Holcombe Blvd. (77225)
713/792-4671
Security: 792-2890
Emergency: 792-HELP (4357)

HOURS
M–F, 8 AM–5 PM
PARKING
Visitors announce themselves at gate
RECEPTION
South entrance hall

The Division of Continuing Education began in 1947 as the University of Texas Postgraduate School of Medicine. The present organization has evolved since that time to provide continuing education for all professionals involved in health sciences.

The division is dedicated to improving and assuring the quality of health care at the community level throughout the state of Texas by providing up-to-date educational programs for those involved in maintaining health.

Besides offering short courses and seminars on many topics, the division acts as a support unit for continuing education of the entire UT Houston Health Science Center.

Continuing Education works with and aids the other UTHSCH facilities in instructing the general public in such areas as prevention of illness and injury, early disease detection through self-knowledge, increased compliance with management plans, and cost-effective use of health care services. There has been a close involvement with activities of the School of Public Health, as well as local agencies and other academic institutions.

The division also participates in hundreds of hospital educational projects. Records have been maintained for some 7,500 attendees at training sessions over a single nine-month period.

The division has worked closely with UT/TV to offer accredited live and videotaped series to physicians and nurses. The alliance of UT/TV and Continuing Education is strengthening and expanding with demands for additional instruction.

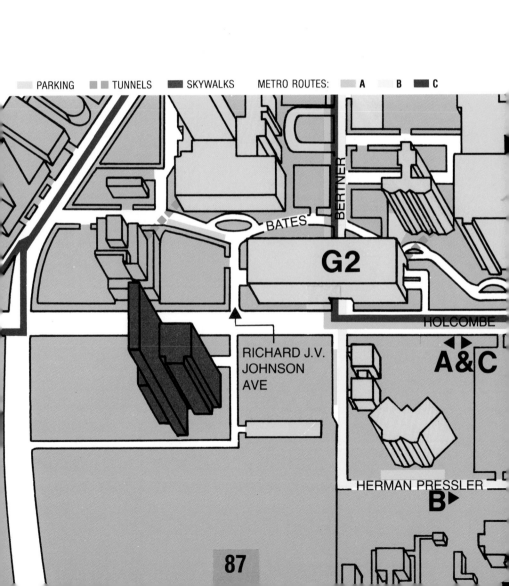

PARKING ■ ■ TUNNELS ■ ■ SKYWALKS METRO ROUTES: ■ **A** ■ **B** ■ **C**

BERTNER

BATES

G2

HOLCOMBE

RICHARD J.V.
JOHNSON
AVE

A&C

HERMAN PRESSLER

B▶

THE UNIVERSITY OF TEXAS HEALTH SCIENCE CENTER AT HOUSTON
GRADUATE SCHOOL OF BIOMEDICAL SCIENCES

6201 Bertner Ave. (77225)
713/792-4750
Security: 792-2890
Emergency: 792-HELP (4357)

HOURS
M–F, 8:30 AM–5 PM
PARKING
Garage #2; limited spaces by building
RECEPTION
First floor

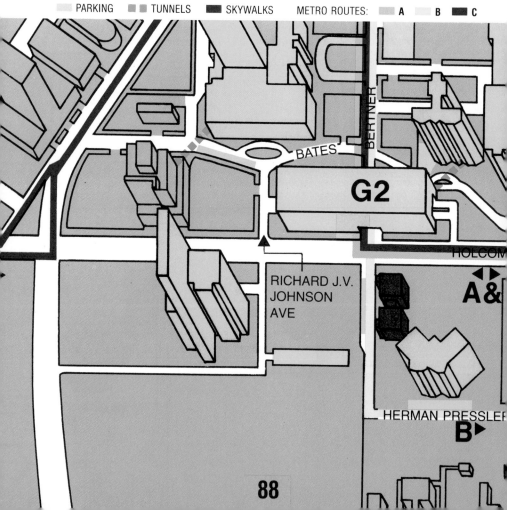

PARKING   TUNNELS   SKYWALKS   METRO ROUTES: A   B   C

BERTNER

BATES

G2

HOLCOM

RICHARD J.V.
JOHNSON
AVE

A&

HERMAN PRESSLER

B▶

The Graduate School of Biomedical Sciences (GSBS) was established in 1963 by the University of Texas Board of Regents to provide opportunities for students to prepare for research and teaching careers in the biomedical sciences through master of science and doctor of philosophy degrees. By special arrangement, the Ph.D. may be combined with an M.D. degree program.

While the majority of students enroll in the M.S./Ph.D program, there are also specialized master's degree plans for those interested in acquiring technical skills in a specific area. Qualified individuals who wish to take advanced courses may enroll as nondegree students.

GSBS provides students the opportunity to fashion an individualized program of study and research in almost any area of biomedical sciences. Fields of investigation include, but are not limited to, anatomy, biochemistry, biomathematics, biomedical communication, biomedical engineering, biophysics, cell biology, endocrinology, genetics, immunology, medical physics, microbiology, molecular biology, neuroscience, nuclear medicine, nutrition, pathology, pharmacology, physiology, reproductive biology, sensory sciences, toxicology, and virology.

In addition to the vast resources of the Medical Center available to GSBS students, there are opportunities for study at the University of Texas System Cancer Center Science Park in Smithville, where the main research interest is in examining cancer-causing agents in the environment. GSBS also has an exchange arrangement with King's College, London.

The graduate faculty is composed of more than three hundred scientists, most of whom are located either in the UT Medical School or at M. D. Anderson Hospital and Tumor Institute; others have their primary appointments directly in GSBS or in other UTHSCH schools. Thus, the faculty provides an academic core for biomedical researchers at the University of Texas at Houston. As a result of its size, diversity, and interest in graduate education, this faculty provides high quality instruction as well as a great deal of individual attention to a student body of about two hundred.

Another facet of GSBS is its research centers, developed as an integral part of the program, whose mission is to make substantial contributions to the body of knowledge of a specific area of biomedical science.

The Sensory Sciences Center deals in the processes of vision, hearing, chemical senses, learning, and memory. Current research at this center includes investigations in color vision, animal psychophysics and behavior, visual neuro-physiology, auditory neurophysiology, chemical senses, and sensory neurochemistry.

The Center for Demographic and Population Genetics seeks a better understanding of the nature and extent of hereditary disease and disability. Research at this center focuses on the factors that contribute to short- and long-term changes in genes, and genotype and phenotype frequencies.

The Medical Genetics Center combines many aspects of genetics—biochemical, clinical, developmental, human population, immunological, and molecular. Current research is focused on molecular variation at the DNA level in human disease, carcinogen testing, and immunogenetics.

The Laboratory for Cyclic Nucleotide Research conducts studies involving the actions of hormones mediated by cyclic nucleotides. Current research involves desensitization of cells by hormones and drugs and mechanisms of hormone action.

The Institute for Technology Development and Assessment, incorporating research centers in cryobiology, bioprocessing, and neurophysiology, provides a structure within which researchers may cross school and disciplinary lines on projects of mutual interest as well as explore opportunities for research and marketing with venture capital concerns.

LIBRARY FACILITIES
A specialized library provides resource material for course work and research.

GENERAL INFORMATION
Graduate research assistantships for first-year students are administered through the Office of the Dean. Requests for a current catalog or information on application should be made to the Registrar's Office at 792-7444.

The Graduate Student Association is an active organization, which enhances the interaction of students with the school, provides social activities, and is involved in service to the community. An annual workshop for area high school science teachers is organized and presented by the association.

6431 Fannin St. (77225)
713/792-2121
Security: 792-2890
Emergency: 792-HELP (4357)

HOURS
M–F, 8 AM–5 PM
PARKING
Garage #4; Hermann Professional Bldg. garage
RECEPTION
Ross Sterling Ave. entrance

The University of Texas Medical School at Houston was organized because of a shortage of doctors, a greater number of qualified applicants than existing medical schools could admit, and the availability of extraordinary and underutilized resources in the Texas Medical Center.

In 1969 the state legislature approved money for the initial costs of the school. Within a year, a dean was appointed and an office opened in the Medical Center. Faculty and staff were recruited, a curriculum was designed, and equipment was assembled. Renovation of existing facilities and new construction were begun. Major construction was completed in 1978.

Thirty-two first-year students were enrolled at the Houston campus by June 1971, and in June 1973 the Medical School graduated a class of twenty-two physicians, most of whom had transferred from University of Texas medical schools in Galveston, Dallas, and San Antonio. The Medical School has grown into a respected institution for medical education and research. About two hundred first-year students are admitted annually.

The primary objective of the Medical School is to train able, responsible physicians to practice in Texas. The four-year curriculum gives each student an opportunity to acquire the intellectual, attitudinal, and manual skills necessary to practice medicine. It teaches the knowledge and use of available resources; provides a base for evaluation of information; urges responsibility, compassion, and empathy for patients; stresses the ideals of medicine and ethical practice; and demands a continuing curiosity. UT Medical School strives to prepare its graduates for practicing medicine in an increasingly complex technological, social, ethical, and economic environment.

PARKING ■■ TUNNELS ■■ SKYWALKS METRO ROUTES: ■ A ■ B ■■ C

HERMANN PARK

OUTER BELT DRIVE

SOUTH MAIN

HERMANN GARAGE

FANNIN

ROSS STERLING

G3

G4

BEN TAUB GARAGE

M.D. ANDERSON

BELLOWS

E. CULLEN

▲A

★ POLICE

91

A medical school can be no better than its patient care programs. Clinical training is designed to teach excellent, understanding medical treatment. Physicians, medical students, and support personnel work together as a team to provide the finest health care available.

The nine-story Medical School building adjoins the Freeman Building and bridges Ross Sterling Avenue (at Entrance #1) to connect with Hermann Hospital. Hermann is its primary teaching hospital, where students receive a major portion of their clinical experience.

Because of its Medical Center affiliations, the school offers many clinical and research opportunities. M. D. Anderson Hospital and Tumor Institute, the Speech and Hearing Institute, and other UTHSCH units are included in Medical School training. Instruction is also available at Shriners Hospital for Crippled Children, St. Joseph Hospital, Memorial Hospital System, St. Anthony Center, San Jose Clinic, and Brackenridge Hospital in Austin.

Additionally, fourth-year medical students are encouraged to broaden their clinical education away from Houston, in positions ranging from family practice in rural communities to clerkships in major teaching hospitals.

Many of the Medical School's research and clinical programs are known worldwide. Experimentation and inquiry are obligatory elements of medical education, and the school has become a recognized leader in research. Recently, fifteen faculty members with appointments in the Medical School and the Graduate School of Biomedical Sciences were named among the world's one thousand most-cited authors of scientific papers. The number of authors at the Medical School is third largest in the country, following Harvard Medical School and the University of California at San Francisco.

The Medical School provides continuing education for its students, graduates, and others throughout their careers to ensure that they have the most current information to maintain their professional quality.

FOOD SERVICE
The cafeteria is located on the ground floor of the Medical School off the Ross Sterling breezeway. It serves breakfast and lunch from 7:00 AM to 2:00 PM, Monday through Friday.

SHOPPING FACILITIES
A gift shop is located in the John H. Freeman Building, ground floor, and is open Monday through Friday, 8:30 AM to 4:30 PM. Besides texts, school supplies, and office materials, it has paperback books, magazines, T-shirts, gifts, and sundries.

LIBRARY FACILITIES
The Medical School has its own specialized Resource Center (ground floor), which provides material for course work and research. Equipment and materials for self-learning programs are available. Students and staff also have the use of other libraries in the Medical Center.

The UT Neuroscience Library, located on the seventh floor of the Medical School building, is one of the two libraries (the other is Baylor College of Medicine's Otorhinolaryngology Library) under contract to Houston Academy of Medicine–TMC Library for the provision of library services. A professional librarian is available for reference, computer data base searches, cataloging, book and journal acquisitions, and management.

The library, supported by the departments of neurology, neurobiology and anatomy, neurosurgery, and ophthalmology, has a five-hundred-volume collection. It provides on-site access for clinicians who need immediate patient-care information.

GENERAL INFORMATION
Applications to the UT Medical School in Houston should be sent to Central Application Center, Suite 102, 210 West 6th Street, Austin, TX 78701.

Medical School employment is handled through UTHSCH Human Resources and Employee Relations, on the first floor of the Houston Main Building. That office may be reached at 792-4290. Questions about residency (housestaff) positions at the Medical School should be sent to the Office of the Associate Dean, Room G.020 (792-5858).

THE UNIVERSITY OF TEXAS HEALTH SCIENCE CENTER AT HOUSTON
MENTAL SCIENCES INSTITUTE

1300 Moursund Ave. (77225)
713/797-0792
Security: 792-2890
Emergency: 792-HELP (4357)

HOURS
M–F, 8 AM–5 PM
PARKING
Garage #6; Garage #5
RECEPTION
Entrance

The University of Texas Mental Sciences Institute was created by the legislature in September 1985 to provide research and to offer treatment in the field of mental health and mental illness.

The institute is the main research facility for the department of psychiatry and behavioral sciences at the UT Medical School and the Harris County Psychiatric Center.

Comprehensive psychiatric outpatient and in-patient services are provided for children, adolescents, and adults. The institute's multidisciplinary staff includes psychiatrists, psychologists, nurses, and social workers. Whether patients are children or the elderly, each receives individual and special attention from the institute's team of experts.

Among special programs offered by the institute is the Child, Adolescent, and Family Clinic, which treats children under 18 with personality disorders, attention deficit disorders, and difficulties stemming from physical handicaps, child abuse, and psychosomatic problems.

Other services include the Developmental Disabilities Center, which treats those with mental and/or physical impairments that limit their functioning at optimal levels. A Chronic Disorders Clinic handles individuals diagnosed as schizophrenic, and the Adult Outpatient Clinic offers psychiatric diagnosis and treatment for adults.

The Gerontology Center provides psychiatric services to senior citizens with emotional, memory, psychosocial, and behavioral problems. The institute's Addictive Behavior Treatment and Research Center treats and counsels alcohol and drug addicts.

Applied clinical research areas of special interest include studies in mental retardation (particularly Down's syndrome), geriatrics, alcoholism, and drug abuse.

FOOD SERVICE
A snack bar/lunchroom with vending machines is on the first floor.

LIBRARY FACILITIES
The library offers an extensive collection of reference materials on psychiatry and mental sciences. Training and teaching videotapes are provided to students, staff, and other institutions. The library is also open to the public from 8:00 AM to 7:00 PM, Monday through Friday.

GUIDED TOURS
While all are welcome, special attention is given to professional visitors and school children in groups. Tours must be arranged in advance.

VOLUNTEERS
The UT Psychiatry Volunteer Corps (791-6800) guides those willing to give their time and effort to the various programs. In addition to working in the clinics and several research sections, volunteers organize recreation activities for patients.

GENERAL INFORMATION
Patients may be self-referred or sent from other agencies, physicians, or therapists. Payment is based on the ability of the individual and family to pay.

THE UNIVERSITY OF TEXAS HEALTH SCIENCE CENTER AT HOUSTON
SCHOOL OF ALLIED HEALTH SCIENCES

6437 Fannin St. (77225)
713/792-4466
Security: 792-2890
Emergency: 792-HELP (4357)

HOURS
M–F, 8 AM–5 PM
PARKING
Garage #4; Hermann Professional Bldg.
garage
RECEPTION
Ground floor

PARKING TUNNELS SKYWALKS METRO ROUTES. A B C

HERMANN PARK

OUTER BELT DRIVE

SOUTH MAIN

HERMANN GARAGE

FANNIN

ROSS STERLING

G4

BEN TAUB GARAGE

G3

M.D. ANDERSON

BELLOWS

E. CULLEN

▲A

★ POLICE

The School of Allied Health Sciences, established in 1973, is charged with developing educational programs to prepare personnel to contribute to health care in various allied health fields. "Allied health fields" refers to all occupations that perform specialized activities in administering health and medical care by augmenting and complementing the practice of physicians, dentists, nurses, public health professionals, and research scientists.

Allied health workers are employed in hospitals, clinics, medical and dental offices, long-term care facilities, labs, public health institutions, schools for special populations, industries, and government installations. These personnel aid in diagnosis, treatment, rehabilitation, and health maintenance.

The school provides quality vocational education training. It is also dedicated to developing and disseminating new knowledge and to providing community service. Its research and curriculum reflect current health care needs, and special attention is paid to recruitment of students who will practice in fields where a shortage of trained workers exists.

Radiologic technology was the first program to be implemented by the school. It was followed by studies in medical technology, biomedical communications, nurse anesthesia, respiratory therapy, nutrition and dietetics, and perfusion technology.

The school has access to many outstanding clinical resources in the Medical Center, in other traditional environments, and in some nontraditional environments. The primary clinical affiliations are with Hermann Hospital and M. D. Anderson Hospital and Tumor Institute. In addition, students receive training in and around Houston at other large hospitals, in community clinics, and in private practices.

Over two hundred volunteer (without salary) faculty, who hold professional positions in hospitals, other academic institutions, clinics, agencies, and private practice, contribute time and expertise to the school. This contribution includes lab and clinical supervision, as well as the teaching of courses. Other volunteer faculty members serve on program advisory committees. All are chosen for their knowledge and skills in a particular field.

Because the programs begin at different entry levels, students may select courses of study appropriate to their backgrounds. A high school diploma is necessary for radiologic technology and respiratory therapy. Other disciplines, such as nutrition, respiratory therapy leadership, medical technology, and perfusion, require two to three years of college. A bachelor's degree is needed for studies in biomedical communications and nurse anesthesia. The Division of Interdisciplinary Studies for the school often brings together students from different fields for the purpose of acquiring skills necessary for, and common to, several programs. Courses last from fifteen weeks to four years.

Faculty-student interaction is emphasized at the school. Pupils receive a large amount of individual instruction and attention, which may explain why graduates perform well on standardized registry exams and have been highly successful in obtaining employment.

The school continues to monitor and adapt to changes in allied health fields. As a discipline evolves, new programs are added or existing courses are modified. The major emphasis remains on educating qualified allied health professionals. At the same time, the school continues to strengthen its contributions to the professional community through faculty research, and to the public through community service activities.

The school prides itself on maintaining state-of-the-art technology. Computers are used extensively in instruction. Teaching and research resources include an oxygen-powered mechanical cardiopulmonary resuscitation device, a computerized pulmonary function laboratory, a Zeiss microscope with digital analyzer, a bomb calorimeter, an atomic absorption-spectrophotometer, a refrigerated room, and a computer-controlled video system.

GUIDED TOURS
The school offers tours of teaching sites, in the Freeman Building and in clinics, to prospective students, teachers, counselors, and so on.

GENERAL INFORMATION
The school offers courses in cardiopulmonary resuscitation to the community and phlebotomy to eligible students. The Community Nutrition and Dietetics Program also provides nutritional counseling on a fee-for-service basis.

Application forms and additional information may be obtained from the Office of the Registrar, UTHSCH, 1100 Holcombe Blvd., Suite 533, P.O. Box 20036, Houston, TX 77225-0036, 713/792-7444. General questions may be answered by calling the dean's office at the School of Allied Health Sciences, 792-4466.

THE UNIVERSITY OF TEXAS HEALTH SCIENCE CENTER AT HOUSTON
SCHOOL OF NURSING

1100 Holcombe Blvd. (77225)
713/792-7800
Security: 792-2890
Emergency: 792-HELP (4357)

HOURS
M–F, 8 AM–5 PM
PARKING
Visitors announce themselves at gate
RECEPTION
Fifth floor

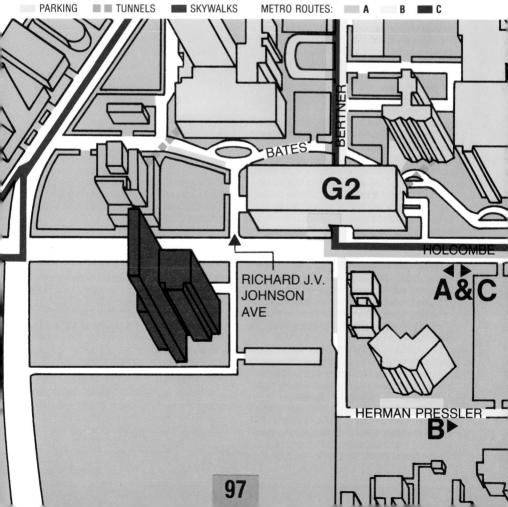

PARKING   TUNNELS   SKYWALKS   METRO ROUTES: A   B   C

BERTNER

BATES

G2

HOLCOMBE

RICHARD J.V. JOHNSON AVE

A&C

HERMAN PRESSLER

B▶

The School of Nursing is one of the oldest nursing schools in the Southwest. Established in 1890 as a function of John Sealy Hospital in Galveston, it was transferred to the University of Texas in 1896 and became a division of the UT Medical Branch on the island.

Until 1957, the school offered a diploma program. Since that time, however, all undergraduate work is channeled toward attainment of a bachelor of science nursing degree (B.S.N.) or the master of science degree (M.S.N.).

In 1960, the school expanded its activities by opening an extension on the UT Austin campus. In 1967, the institution was reorganized as the University of Texas School of Nursing, system wide, and administrative offices were moved to Austin. In 1972, it was renamed the University of Texas System School of Nursing. Senior and junior courses were offered in Houston and five other cities around the state. In 1976, the UT Board of Regents placed each school under the administration of the president of the health science center or academic institution nearest its location.

The nursing school offers high-quality educational courses for both graduate and undergraduate students. Major contributions have been made in nursing science through research. The school actively provides service programs that enhance health care in the community and participates in local, state, and national organizations directed to the nursing profession.

The educational effort includes extensive classroom work in nursing theory as well as hands-on clinical practice. Lecture classes are held on the fourth floor of the Main Building. Clinical classes are conducted in facilities throughout the Medical Center. This training prepares nurses to act as colleagues with fellow professionals in delivering exemplary health care.

A superior faculty of fifty individuals handles theoretical and practical training. An experienced teacher is present in all clinical situations to give instruction and, if needed, assistance. The faculty of the undergraduate program has been active in developing nursing clinics in the Houston area and is engaged in a pilot project using television to improve instruction.

Future development plans assure that participation by the faculty in nursing practice, as a service to the community and a mechanism for growth, will continue. Additional emphasis is being placed on capabilities to conduct nursing research.

Requirements for admission are strict, based on specific criteria. Students enjoy a variety of educational opportunities. Clinical learning experiences are available at Hermann Hospital, the UT System Cancer Center, St. Luke's Episcopal Hospital, Texas Children's Hospital, Texas Heart Institute, and Texas Institute for Rehabilitation and Research, as well as the Memorial Hospital System. Additional experience can be gained in neighborhood health centers, nursing homes, day care centers, county and city health departments, mental health facilities, physicians' offices, and clinics throughout the Houston area.

The school is ranked annually by the American Association of Colleges of Nursing and now offers six areas of specialization in its master's program: nurse anesthesia, critical care, perinatal, emergency, oncological, and gerontological nursing.

About three hundred students are currently enrolled. Of these, over half are in the program leading to a B.S. in Nursing. The balance are registered nurses earning their B.S. through a flexible course, which allows them to work while furthering their education. Some students attend classes but are not active in a degree program.

A full array of the latest teaching and diagnostic equipment is available in the school, including an audiovisual production center and projection TV systems.

As the School of Nursing completed its centennial year of operation, new programs, increased efforts in research, and strong emphasis on caring outreach keep the institution in the forefront of nursing as it fulfills its role of service to the profession and the community.

FOOD SERVICE

A cafeteria on the second floor serves breakfast and lunch from 7:30 AM to 2:30 PM, Monday through Friday. Vending machines are available on the sixth and seventh floors. A confectionery is located on the first floor.

LIBRARY FACILITIES

A Learning Resource Center on the fourth floor of the Main Building contains nursing journals, texts and references, and an audiovisual department.

GENERAL INFORMATION

Inquiries concerning qualifications and prerequisites for admission to the school, as well as brochures, catalogs for undergraduate and graduate courses, registration dates, and academic calendars, may be had by contacting the UTHSCH Central Registrar's Office at 792-8525.

THE UNIVERSITY OF TEXAS HEALTH SCIENCE CENTER AT HOUSTON
SCHOOL OF PUBLIC HEALTH

1200 Herman Pressler Blvd. (77225)
713/792-4425
Security: 792-2890
Emergency: 792-HELP (4357)

HOURS
M–F, 8 AM–5 PM
PARKING
Garage #2; limited spaces in front of building
RECEPTION
Room W130

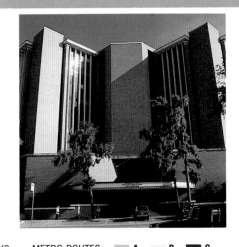

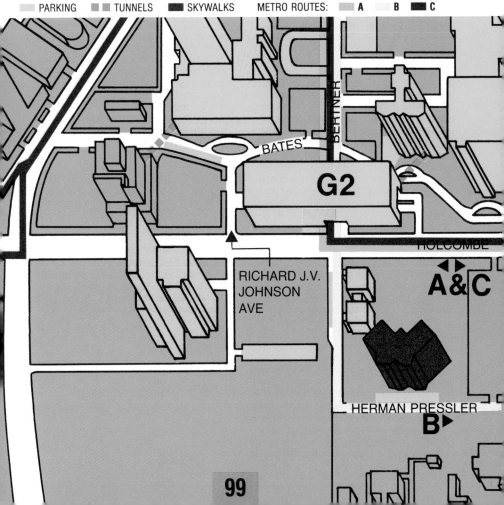

PARKING　　TUNNELS　　SKYWALKS　　METRO ROUTES:　A　B　C

BERLINER

BATES

G2

HOLCOMBE

RICHARD J.V.
JOHNSON
AVE

A & C

HERMAN PRESSLER
B ▶

The School of Public Health is the only graduate school of public health in Texas. It is one of twenty-three in the United States accredited by the Council on Education for Public Health.

This graduate-level school provides education and training for students who will assume careers dedicated to preventing diseases and disabilities in populations as large as whole cities or as small as a group of industrial employees.

A school of public health was authorized within the University of Texas system in 1947, but it was not realized until 1967, when public-spirited citizens appealed to the legislature and appropriations were made. Its first class began in 1969 in rented and borrowed space. Enrollment doubled the next year, and again the year after that.

In 1976, the school moved into its ten-story twin towers in the Medical Center. Since that time, hundreds have earned masters and doctoral degrees. Currently, the school graduates about one hundred persons each year. Of all the UT Health Science Center's schools, it has the highest percentage of foreign nationals.

Graduates work in most states in the United States and in dozens of foreign countries. More than a third of those who have completed degrees are employed by government agencies; another third in academic institutions. Others have jobs in private industry and voluntary health organizations.

The school offers four degrees and many fields of study but no undergraduate programs. Students include physicians, dentists, nurses, educators, administrators, microbiologists, architects, engineers, pharmacists, nutritionists, and others. Courses range from a few months to four years.

A master of public health (M.P.H.) is the basic professional degree in this field. The doctor of public health (Dr. P.H.) degree is designed for those who choose careers in teaching, research, or professional leadership.

Study and research plans include community health practice, disease control, health services organization, international and rural health, occupational health/aerospace medicine, population studies and nutrition, and urban health.

The school also has programs leading to master of science and doctor of philosophy degrees in community health sciences. Special courses in biometry (development of statistical models for quantitative analysis of biological systems), behavioral sciences, environmental sciences, epidemiology, and human ecology are offered.

Public health encompasses many areas of medicine and related fields, including the social sciences. Students survey broad areas but are expected to concentrate their studies and research in one or, at most, a few subjects. An interdisciplinary curriculum assures a proper subject balance in each program.

The school has created four specialized divisions. The Institute of Environmental Health is concerned with the effects of our environment on human health. The Human Nutrition Center works to solve nutrition problems and promotes nutrition education for professionals and the public. The Epidemiology Center focuses on advanced studies in disease prevention. The Center for Health and Manpower Policy Studies was established to make data available as a resource for legislators and other policy makers in considering health policy alternatives for state government.

A special program in San Antonio was established in 1979. Fields of study there center on communicable disease problems of South Central Texas, as well as international and occupational health.

Besides offering postgraduate education, the Epidemiology Center attracts distinguished visiting scientists who wish to pursue scholarly work. The center sponsors conferences, seminars, and workshops on topics of interest and importance in disease prevention. The school is known as a major resource for teaching, research, and service in epidemiology. It is in constant communication with professionals in public health practice to improve awareness of recent advances and to be sure that teaching and research remain relevant to community problems.

LIBRARY FACILITIES

The library maintains an extensive collection of books, journals, documents, audiocassettes, microfilms, and other materials. Visitors may enjoy the leisure reading area in the library, located on the first floor.

GENERAL INFORMATION

The school offers computer and audiovisual facilities and services to all faculty and students. It owns and operates a Boston whaleboat at Galveston Bay, which is used for studies on ecology of the Texas Gulf Coast.

THE UNIVERSITY OF TEXAS HEALTH SCIENCE CENTER AT HOUSTON SPEECH AND HEARING INSTITUTE

1343 Moursund Ave. (77225)
713/792-4601
Security: 792-2890
Emergency: 792-HELP (4357)

HOURS
M–F, 8 AM–5 PM
PARKING
Garage #6; limited spaces in adjacent lot
RECEPTION
Parking-lot entrance

PARKING ▓▓ TUNNELS ▓▓ SKYWALKS METRO ROUTES: ▓▓ A ░░ B ▓▓ C

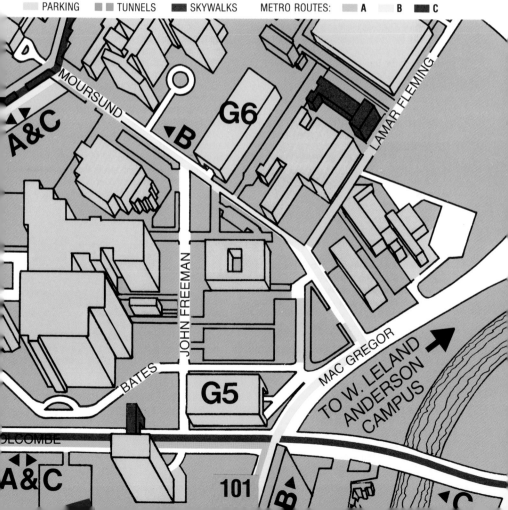

One of every ten Americans suffers a speech, language, or hearing problem. Communication disorders are the No. 1 handicapping disability in the United States. Studies show that more people have hearing, speech, and language impairments than heart disease, paralysis, epilepsy, blindness, cerebral palsy, TB, muscular dystrophy, and multiple sclerosis *combined*. Approximately 23 percent of persons between ages 60 and 65 have diminished hearing.

In the 1940s, a committee of medical and civic-minded citizens recognized that only minimal services were available to communicatively handicapped children and adults in Houston. In 1950, Jack L. Bangs, Ph.D., and Tina E. Bangs, Ph.D., were appointed director and assistant director of a speech-language-hearing program.

By 1951, the Houston Speech and Hearing Center was in operation in basement space donated by Methodist Hospital. Rapid expansion required additional room. The center rented a house on Crawford Street for its speech-language therapy clinic. With gifts and grants, a building was erected for the center in the Texas Medical Center in 1959. In 1969, a second building was dedicated.

To take advantage of state funding for teaching and research, the center became affiliated with the University of Texas System in 1971 as a Division of Communication Disorders in the Graduate School of Biomedical Sciences. When UT formed its Health Science Center at Houston, the center was separated from the graduate school and its name was changed to the Speech and Hearing Institute.

The institute's three goals are to provide teaching, research, and clinical services in human communication and its disorders. Education and research are administered by the Division of Academic and Research Affairs, and the Division of Clinical Services helps communicatively handicapped individuals.

A master of science degree in communication sciences is offered through the Graduate School of Biomedical Sciences. Students receive training and instruction from faculty drawn from the institute, schools in UTHSCH, and other institutions in the Medical Center, as well as Rice University and the University of Houston.

The institute offers advanced capabilities in research into the biomedical aspects of language learning and language disorders. Efforts are focused on basic and clinical information that will help in solving problems that interfere with language and language learning. Experimentation is conducted in laboratories, sound-treated rooms, and an echo-free chamber. Researchers also make use of a TV studio, photo and X-ray labs, computers, and machine and electronics shops.

Because the institute is funded in part by the United Way, outpatient clinical services are available to citizens of Harris, Fort Bend, and Montgomery counties on a sliding fee scale. It is open to all children and adults with speech, language, and/or hearing disorders.

Speech language pathologists help children with language disorders, defective articulation, and cleft palates. Adults whose ability to speak has been impaired because of stroke, head injury, or illness are also treated. Many individuals require voice rehabilitation or instruction in speaking after removal of the larynx. Audiologists work with those who have hearing deficits.

Diagnostic and treatment services are provided in the Medical Center at the institute (outpatients only), Hermann Hospital, Institute for Rehabilitation and Research, and Hermann Professional Building. Outside the Medical Center, clinical services are available at the Richmond State School for the Retarded, Northside Health Clinic, San Jose Health Clinic, and other centers, as well as through areawide screening services.

The institute has been undergoing reorganization and restructuring of its clinical services to take advantage of new technology. Innovative approaches to the evaluation and treatment of communication disorders through specialty clinics are already showing results.

LIBRARY FACILITIES
The institute, along with the Institute for Rehabilitation and Research, is served by the Information Services Center. This two-thousand-volume library is housed in the Speech and Hearing building. It is for the use of staff and students.

GUIDED TOURS
The institute can arrange a guided tour of its facilities by appointment.

VOLUNTEERS
The institute has a volunteer Advisory Board, whose members are appointed by the president of the Health Science Center. The board disseminates information about institute services in the community. Appointees serve as advocates of the communicatively handicapped and advise the institute on budget and program planning for clinical services.

THE UNIVERSITY OF TEXAS SYSTEM CANCER CENTER
M. D. ANDERSON HOSPITAL AND TUMOR INSTITUTE AT HOUSTON

1515 Holcombe Blvd. (77030)
713/792-2121
Hospital patient information: 792-7000
Security: 792-2890
Emergency: 792-HELP (4357)

HOURS
Clinic: M–F, 8 AM–5 PM
Visiting: 1 PM–8 PM daily (minimum age: 12, except Su, 1–2 PM)
Emergency: 24 hours daily—patients only (792-2310)
PARKING
Garage #2; Garage #5; adjacent surface lots
RECEPTION
Clinic and hospital lobbies

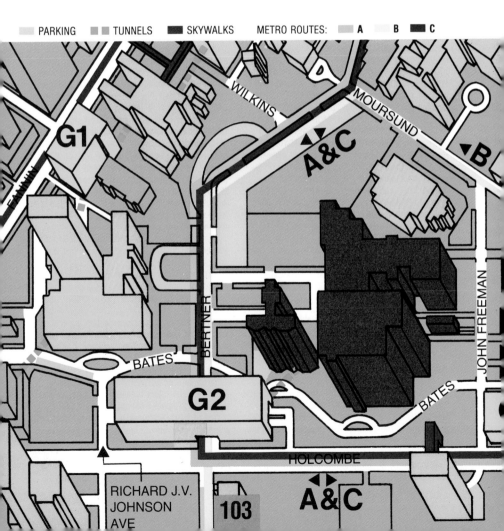

In 1941, the legislature appropriated $500,000 to establish a state cancer research hospital to be administered by the University of Texas. In its first major project, the newly formed M. D. Anderson Foundation offered to match the state funds and provide a site. The offer was accepted and it was decided the hospital should be named after the foundation's late benefactor, Monroe D. Anderson.

The new cancer center spent its developmental years in temporary quarters near downtown Houston before moving in 1954 into its permanent building in the Texas Medical Center. In 1969, facilities were expanded with the addition of the Gimbel Wing and the research-oriented Bates-Freeman Building. In a 1972 reorganization of all University of Texas health-related units, the UT M. D. Anderson complex became a part of the newly formed UT System Cancer Center. In 1976, M. D. Anderson was expanded once again to more than 1.2 million square feet with the additions of the Lutheran Hospital Pavilion, the Clark Clinic Building, a research wing, a radiation therapy center, and a chapel.

Figuring prominently in the cancer institute's success story is Dr. R. Lee Clark. Clark was masterful as the hospital's first director in 1946 and then as its first president in 1968. Clark directed M. D. Anderson for over thirty years, being succeeded as president in 1978 by Dr. Charles A. LeMaistre.

The UT Cancer Center is the official state agency for the care of Texans with cancer, for training and research in cancer, and for activities related to the prevention of the disease. The ultimate goal of the center is the elimination of cancer as a significant health threat in Texas.

Although M. D. Anderson is known worldwide, its primary focus is on the Texas patient. Cancer care is provided for Texas residents regardless of their income. Since taking its first admissions in 1944, the institute has treated more than 175,000 persons from every county in the state. Approximately one-third have been unable to pay and have received care at no cost to themselves. M. D. Anderson is not a charity hospital but charges Texas residents for services according to their financial ability. As one of only twenty comprehensive cancer centers in the country, M. D. Anderson admits many patients from other states and nations, although they must be full-paying.

M. D. Anderson has become one of the world's most widely respected centers for cancer treatment. Annually, there are hundreds of thousands of inpatient and outpatient visits. Since 1947, about seventeen thousand professionals and scientists in related fields have received training here.

Facilities for patient care include the original M. D. Anderson Hospital building, which has 184 beds, and the Lutheran Hospital Pavilion with 330 private rooms. The adjoining Clark Clinic Building can accommodate 1,500 outpatients daily. The Radiotherapy Center treats more than 225 individuals each day. The Rehabilitation Center is the nation's first facility devoted solely to the recovering cancer patient. As major patient care rehabilitation services become focused at the expanded M. D. Anderson Hospital complex, the Rehabilitation Center will become a patient residence. Also part of the complex is the Anderson Mayfair, a patient-family hotel across Holcombe Boulevard. Rotary House International, a fifteen-story hotel, will be connected to the hospital by a closed overhead walkway and will provide special housing for patients and their families.

M. D. Anderson's patient care mission includes prevention, diagnosis, treatment, and rehabilitation. The outpatient clinic is the start of most treatments. M. D. Anderson contains twenty-four outpatient clinic stations, divided according to specialty and site of disease, including a children's facility. In the clinics, the patient's disease is diagnosed and the best course of action is decided. The Cancer Center has completed the first two floors of its new outpatient facilities. The ten-floor building is expected to be complete by late 1987. Other renovations have begun to lay the groundwork for future improvements to patient care areas. A seven-story research building has also added much needed space.

One of M. D. Anderson's advantages is its team approach, for often a combination of therapies gives the most successful results. Thus, a patient could undergo surgery to remove the bulk of a tumor, radiotherapy and chemotherapy to kill any remaining cancer cells, and immunotherapy to stimulate the body's own defense mechanisms against a possible recurrence of the cancer.

In 1984, M. D. Anderson adopted a special code of ethical guidelines (the first such statement by a cancer center), which emphasizes the importance of treating cancer patients as individuals, not as research subjects. The code underscores the need to help patients live with their disease and details ten principles, ranging from the value of life to honesty with patients about cancer and costs of treatments.

Vital to patient care is the often overlooked area of emotional support. M. D. Anderson has almost eight hundred trained volunteers providing personal services and attention to patients and their families. The Volunteer Department includes a bilingual volunteer program and personnel specially schooled in translating medical terminology.

Because of its vast size M. D. Anderson is able to offer many services for cancer patients that are unavailable in most general hospitals. Foremost among these is a $5 million cyclotron. The cyclotron is revolutionary because of its ability to bombard with neutrons tumors that are resistant to conventional forms of radiation. Other diagnostic tools include a magnetic resonance imaging unit, which produces extremely detailed images of body organs and systems without radiation.

M. D. Anderson has also pioneered a "protected environment"—a hospital floor containing patient rooms equipped with special air filters designed to reduce the incidence of airborne bacteria, important for those who are germ-sensitive because they are undergoing chemotherapy.

Another innovation is the pain clinic, working to reduce any pain the postoperative patient may encounter. A full-time psychiatry service is also available for the purpose of combating postoperative depression and emotional problems. Also quite important in cancer treatment is self-confidence and esteem. A technique has been perfected to allow "permanent" attachment of artificial face parts for those who have had disfiguring cancer surgery.

Outpatient clinics are being expanded, as are medical programs designed to lessen therapy that requires hospitalization. The goal is to allow patients to be treated at home rather than in the clinic, or in the clinic instead of the hospital.

M. D. Anderson's second focus is research. The hospital is known throughout the world as a research center in basic and clinical sciences. As in patient care, the research labs do much of their work in interdisciplinary teams, made possible by the cancer institute's extensive size. (Environmental research is also conducted at the UT Science Park, composed of two units near Bastrop and Smithville.) Another advantage is having the cancer research center located in a hospital that deals with cancer patients; this ensures that research results are incorporated into treatment in a minimal amount of time and, reciprocally, that results can be evaluated immediately for promising new lines of exploration. Studies are always mindful of determining ways to detect cancers at the earliest stage and of finding the best method of cancer treatment.

Although the research center's projects are too numerous to list (more than 500 at this writing), examples include such efforts as the study of biologic response modifiers, substances naturally found within the body that ward off cancer; and experimentation on oncogenes, genes found in human chromosomes that may be responsible for changing normal cells into cancer cells. Cells are probed at the genetic level, including experimentation with gene splicing. M. D. Anderson published the results of the world's first study of leukocyte interferon synthesized by recombinant DNA technology.

The hospital has a preventive medicine clinic for work on the cause and cure of acquired immune deficiency syndrome (AIDS). A center has been formally established for investigative work in radiology; a multidisciplinary program in neuro-oncology is addressing problems associated with cancers of the brain and spinal cord; and a section studies bone marrow for transplantation, growing it *in vitro,* and cleansing it of contaminating tumor cells.

Another program has been undertaken to evaluate the effectiveness of whole-body and regional hyperthermia (the superheating of either tumors or the entire body under anesthesia, using radiowaves or externally applied heat). Many studies are being conducted on large risk factors for salivary gland cancer, testicular cancer, breast cancer, and the relationship between removal of the gall bladder and subsequent development of colon cancer.

Research often translates to immediate patient benefits. Portable pumps, a new method of delivering chemotherapy for some cancers, have given many almost hospital-free lives. Investigators hope to expand the use of these pumps to treatment of many types of cancer and uses, such as delivering painkillers.

M. D. Anderson also furnishes a wide range of educational services. For public education, the UT Cancer Center offers its Cancer Information Service, a bilingual hotline providing Texans with accurate information about cancer prevention, detection, treatment, and rehabilitation, as well as descriptions of services available in the caller's area. (Monday through Friday, business hours: in Houston, 792-3245, or toll-free, 1-800-4-CANCER).

More than 125,000 callers have been assisted by this telephone program. The CancerWISE Community Speakers Bureau provides instruction and talks for various groups upon request (call 792-3363). The institute continues to train nurses from private physicians' offices and community health clinics in the techniques of early cancer detection. Every year several residency programs and clinical trainee fellowships are offered. For high school and college students interested in science and health care, M. D. Anderson provides an eight-week training session each summer.

The institute has sponsored the annual Symposium on Fundamental Cancer Research since 1946 and the annual Clinical Conference on Cancer since 1956 (both published now by the University of Texas Press, Austin) and the annual Pediatric Mental Health Conference since 1976.

FOOD SERVICE
The cafeteria, located on the ground floor between the Lutheran Pavilion and the Clinic Building, provides full service from 6:30 AM to 8:00 PM, Monday through Friday, and from 6:30 AM to 7:00 PM, weekends and holidays. Additionally, a deli service is offered in this cafeteria every day between 11:00 AM and 7:00 PM.

A pleasant atrium garden on the ground floor of the Clinic Building, adjacent to the cafeteria, is open for lunch and dinner. There are tables, chairs, and umbrellas for fresh-air dining. The cafeteria offers a carry-out service with disposable plates, cups, and cartons.

The Rehabilitation Center (2015 Thomas Street) cafeteria, located on the second floor, is open from 11:30 AM to 1:00 PM, Monday through Friday; 7:00 AM to 8:15 AM, 11:30 AM to 1:00 PM, and 4:45 PM to 6:15 PM, weekends and holidays.

SHOPPING FACILITIES
Two gift shops are available to patients, visitors, and guests. The gift shop in the Lutheran Pavilion lobby is open 7:45 AM to 8:45 PM, weekdays, and 8:00 AM to 4:30 PM, weekends. The gift shop in the Clark Clinic lobby is open 7:45 AM to 4:30 PM, weekdays only.

LIBRARY FACILITIES
The Patient/Family Library, a branch of the Houston Public Library, is located just off the Lutheran Pavilion lobby (room LG.009).

Physicians, students, and Medical Center employees have access to M. D. Anderson's Research Medical Library, located on the first floor of the Bates-Freeman Building. It offers an extensive selection on cancer research and catalogs everything written on clinical cancer, including foreign publications. The Research Medical Library is participating in the forthcoming installation of the integrated library system of Medical Center libraries.

RELIGIOUS SERVICES
Ministry at M. D. Anderson includes routine visits to new admissions, response to referrals or special needs, calls on patients prior to surgery, worship services, and participation in discharge planning committees and pain clinic surveillance committees that oversee all research treatments given patients.

Like physicians, chaplains are "on call" 24 hours a day and are always available to a patient or family members. The chaplains represent a broad range of religious denominations and are happy to serve both those of their own faith and those who may have strong religious feelings yet are not connected with any specific faith.

The interdenominational Freeman-Dunn Sanctuary is open for meditation every day. The chapel entrance is on the ground floor of the hospital building, near the cafeteria. Worship services, in English and in Spanish, are held every Sunday in the sanctuary. Sunday morning services are broadcast over closed-circuit television within the hospital.

During the week, Protestant Holy Communion, Mass, scripture readings, prayer, and meditation are held. Friday evenings a Sabbath film is shown over closed-circuit television. Meditation rooms are available on some floors (Lutheran Pavilion floors 2, 5, 8, and 11) and are open at all times.

OVERNIGHT ACCOMMODATIONS
All patient rooms can accommodate a family member for the night. The hospital encourages parents to stay with pediatric patients. In addition, the Anderson Mayfair Hotel is available to patients and families at rates comparable to better hotels in the area.

GUIDED TOURS
Guided tours of the hospital are given Monday through Friday to groups of twenty or less (call 792-3030).

VOLUNTEERS
The hospital has an extensive volunteer program, tailoring assignments to meet the skills and interests of eight hundred volunteers in more than thirty-five patient and nonpatient-contact areas. From working in gift shops to delivering flowers to charting vital signs to researching scientific literature, the volunteers are considered an important part of the health care team. Volunteers range in age from teenagers to senior citizens. More vol-

unteers are always needed. (To volunteer, call 792-7180.)

GENERAL INFORMATION

Hospital volunteers prepare a full schedule of recreational activities for patients. Adults may enjoy selecting a handicraft kit from the volunteer craft cart or checking out videocassette recorders and movie tapes. Patients, their families, and employees are invited to use several family rooms and a solarium.

Pediatric patients are offered bingo games, art classes, teen dinners, parties, movies and popcorn, and an aerobics class for them and their parents.

A beauty shop, located in the basement of the Lutheran Pavilion, is available to patients free of charge.

Fully equipped self-service postal facilities provide convenient mail services for staff, patients, and visitors. Located on the first floor of the Clinic Building and on the third floor of the Houston Main Building, the postal facilities make it easy to buy stamps, postcards, and envelopes and to mail letters and packages 24 hours a day.

A social worker, assigned to each patient at registration, is always available to help with social and emotional needs. The social workers can assist in locating community resources to meet financial problems. Patients may request financial counselors as well.

Patient care coordinators, assigned to each of the clinic stations, ease patients through the system and handle any procedural problems.

Support groups and classes for patients are offered through the Patient Education Office. The classes, taught by hospital professionals, cover topics like catheter care and breast self-examination. Chemotherapy is explained in both Spanish and English. Videotapes of the classes are also made available.

There are two pharmacies for outpatients, one located on the first floor of the new Clinic; the other located immediately inside the old Clinic entrance.

Since 1973, young patients at the hospital have created a collection of Christmas cards as an expression of their hope and happiness. Each year more and more cards have been sold. Proceeds are used for projects and activities for the pediatric patients. Funds help buy school, handicraft, and art supplies; books, records, tapes, and videocassettes; toys and playground equipment. They provide a summer camp program and outings to special events, are used to pay meal chits for financially disadvantaged parents, and provide interpreters for Spanish-speaking patients and families. College scholarships for M. D. Anderson pediatric

patients also have been established. Information is available by calling 792-6266 or writing M. D. Anderson Hospital Volunteer Services.

Those who wish to be treated at M. D. Anderson must have their physicians make the initial contact by letter or phone. Physicians should contact the New Patient Referral Office, 713 / 792-6161. In Texas the toll-free number is 1-800-392-1611. The New Patient Referral Office can answer any questions of prospective patients. Helpline telephones are also available throughout the hospital for information and aid. Just pick up the HELP! phone and ask.

Coin-operated lockers are provided in the Clinic Building lobby. When it rains, a tunnel is opened from the basement of the Lutheran Pavilion to Garage #2. Throughout the M. D. Anderson complex there are HELP! phones on the walls. If you are lost, need directions, or want information, pick up Helpline.

The hospital publishes the bimonthly *Cancer Bulletin,* a journal on cancer treatment and research directed toward the Texas physician who does not treat patients with cancer on a daily basis. It also publishes *Oncolog,* a quarterly publication designed to keep the medical world informed about the latest developments at M. D. Anderson.

Visitors who wish to receive a subscription to *Conquest,* a quarterly magazine about cancer advances for a lay audience, should call 792-3030.

CHECK-IN/CHECK-OUT

First-time patients should allow plenty of time to reach the hospital and find a parking space. They should wear comfortable clothes and bring crafts to work on or reading materials to help pass the time while waiting for appointments. Patients requiring wheelchairs may be dropped off at either of the Clinic entrances, where a wheelchair can be provided.

In order to fill out insurance and financial records, it is necessary for you to have the following:
  Medicare/Medicaid I.D. card
  Blue Cross or other insurance I.D. card
  Military I.D. card if in the U.S. Armed Forces
  Social Security number
  Driver's license

VETERANS ADMINISTRATION MEDICAL CENTER

2002 Holcombe Blvd. (77030)
713/795-4411
Security: 795-7467

HOURS
M–F, 8 AM–4:30 PM
Emergency: 24 hours daily (795-7500)
PARKING
By VA Buildings
RECEPTION
Central VA building lobby

PARKING   TUNNELS   SKYWALKS   METRO ROUTES: A   B   C

The Veterans Administration Medical Center, located about one-half mile from the Texas Medical Center, was originally a naval hospital (1944–1946). The center has fifty buildings and covers more than one hundred acres. The facility, one of the most sizable and complex in the VA system, is now among the largest hospitals in Houston and offers primary, secondary, and tertiary health care to veterans from Texas and neighboring states. It is a district referral center for several specialties.

The Veterans Administration Medical Center in Houston is part of a VA medical district, composed of eight medical centers and four satellite clinics. The VA is committed to providing the best quality care to eligible area veterans. Patients requiring services not available are referred to other VA facilities or contracted to another local tertiary care institution.

The VA Medical Center provides practically every health service to veterans. Nursing home care as well as day treatment, day hospital, and mental hygiene clinics are available. Patients are referred to the Houston center for certain specialties, which include open heart surgery, supervoltage therapy, spinal cord injury, and intraocular lens implants. Other services offered are drug abuse and alcohol dependence treatment programs.

This vast center houses specialized sections, including medical and surgical intensive care units; a geriatrics evaluation and treatment unit; specialized laboratories, including electron microscopy, nuclear medicine, and computerized axial tomography (CT scan); and noninvasive labs where studies with radioactive pharmaceuticals are performed to measure cerebral blood flow. Heat catheterization, coronary angioplasty, echocardiography, and cardiac rehabilitation facilities to care for patients with heart disease are also available.

The VA's hemodialysis unit provides inpatient and home dialysis programs. There is a pulmonary function lab along with a respiratory care center. Other noteworthy divisions are the audiology and speech pathology unit, the prosthetic treatment center, and sleep research laboratories, contributing diagnostic and treatment capabilities to veterans throughout the Southwest.

The Veterans Administration has two outlying service sites—a drug treatment center in downtown Houston and an outpatient clinic in Beaumont.

Seventy-five percent of the VA's patients live in the community or within a thirty-mile radius. Presently there are more than a thousand beds at the center. Over 18,000 patients are admitted annually and nearly 6,000 surgical procedures are carried out. There are approximately 300,000 outpatient visits per year, with well over 13 million lab and 100,000 X-ray examinations. The complex employs over 2,500 people.

The veteran population in the Houston area is growing quickly and the present average age of 53 is expected to reach 57 in 1990. A 14 percent increase in the number of veterans over the age of 65 by 1990 is anticipated, as is a significantly increased demand on the facility. It has been projected that those over age 65 will require health care at five times the rate of those under 65.

This VA Medical Center has close ties to the Medical Center and many medical institutions in the Houston area. It is primarily affiliated with Baylor College of Medicine and is associated with the University of Texas Dental Branch. It is closely allied with five separate nursing schools and is involved in residency training for several clinical programs. The VA has had a close relationship with a number of Medical Center institutions for decades and became a member institution in 1985.

The educational institutions affiliated with the VA contribute to a well-balanced instructional program. The VA's association with Baylor functions through a dean's committee. Regular staff members, consultants, and attending physicians are chosen by the committee and most have faculty appointments at Baylor. Conferences and ward rounds are conducted for each service at the VA.

There are 141 residents engaged in such specialties as dentistry, dermatology, family practice, internal medicine, neurology, neurosurgery, nuclear medicine, ophthalmology, orthopedic surgery, otolaryngology, pathology, physical medicine, plastic surgery, psychiatry, diagnostic radiology, radiotherapy, general surgery, thoracic surgery, and urology. Teaching medical students is part of their regimen.

There is also a wide range of training for the allied health professions. This VA unit is affiliated with five schools in audiology and speech pathology and five schools in nursing, nurse anesthesiology, and related fields. Instruction in allied health care includes dietetics, medical technology, nuclear medicine, pharmacy, physician assistants, psychology, and social work, as well as corrective, occupational, and physical therapies and health care administration.

Research at the center is among the most active in the national health system. There are currently thirty-seven principal investigators whose efforts are centered in such categories as sleep and sexual function, alcoholism and drug addiction, coronary artery and pulmonary diseases, endocrinology, spinal cord, and oncology.

The center assumes a leading role in state and local health and public service groups. It is represented on numerous national committees, and many of the professional staff have international exposure. Its service organizations are active and supportive.

Expansion has been piecemeal over the years, and many of the buildings are outmoded and unable to be remodeled to correct operational, safety, and patient privacy deficiencies. Construction on a total replacement facility was begun in 1986. It is located behind the present facility. Upon completion of the hospital, the existing facility will be torn down and made into a commons area. The new 927-bed facility and a 120-bed nursing home care unit projected for 1990 will ensure modern, effective, efficient health care for veterans, who now include an increasing number of elderly and female ex-service personnel. Patient rooms will accommodate two to four beds, eliminating the present ward system.

Plans for the replacement project incorporate nuclear magnetic resonance imaging; a linear accelerator; major expansion of facilities for spinal cord injuries; increasing the nursing home care capacity; establishment of an intermediate care medical bed section; a stepped-up geriatric care program, to cover a geriatric care evaluation unit, a psychogeriatric unit, a geriatric day hospital, and a geriatric day care consortium; instituting a residential care program; and creating a substance abuse halfway house.

FOOD SERVICE
A cafeteria is located on the second floor of the central building. Hot entrées are served through lunch, with sandwiches and light meals available afterward. Open 7:00 AM to 4:00 PM, Monday through Friday; 8:00 AM to 2:30 PM, Saturday and Sunday.

SHOPPING FACILITIES
The canteen is a retail store, open from 7:30 AM to 4:00 PM, Monday through Friday; 8:00 AM to 2:30 PM Saturday and Sunday. Besides drugstore items, such as cigarettes, candies, toiletries, pens, watches, radios, and cameras, it also sells snacks, clothing, suits, shoes, and a small amount of women's apparel.

LIBRARY FACILITIES
The VA library, located in the central building, is divided into two sections: a medical library, with references, texts, and journals for physicians, nurses, and students; and a leisure library for patients, with newspapers, magazines, and books. Library personnel also make rounds of wards with a selection of reading matter.

RELIGIOUS SERVICES
Four full-time and four part-time chaplains are on call at all times. A chapel in the central building is open from 7:00 AM to 9:00 PM daily. Catholic services are held daily and Protestant services are given on Sundays.

GUIDED TOURS
Because of busy schedules, public tours are not normally given except on special occasions, such as the February 14 "Salute to Hospitalized Veterans."

VOLUNTEERS
The VA relies on its more than one thousand volunteers, who represent civic, veteran, fraternal, welfare, church, and youth organizations. These volunteers contribute over 100,000 work hours each year.

GENERAL INFORMATION
Recreation and leisure services include a gymnasium, basketball court, six-lane bowling alley, hobby / craft room, music room, and game room with electronic games and pool tables. There is also a 1,000-seat movie auditorium.

Veterans receive medical services free, but social workers can assist in many other areas. They can suggest community resources for those who may not be eligible for certain veterans programs but need special aid. Their arrangements are as varied as the requests—from transportation for an appointment to locating a halfway house for a graduate of the alcohol or drug treatment programs.

A pharmacy provides free prescriptions to eligible veterans.

Eligibility questions should be directed to the Eligibility Unit at 795-7405.

CHECK-IN/CHECK-OUT
Admittance is on a walk-in basis. Appointments are not scheduled for first-time patients. Veterans must go to the central building, where they will be directed to Admitting/Receiving. To determine eligibility for treatment, all are asked to bring honorable discharge papers or, if one is service connected, a copy of those papers or patient data card, plus identification and proof of residence. For additional admittance information, call 795-7412.

Two certified police departments operate in the Texas Medical Center. Most individual institutions also have their own security personnel.

Texas Medical Center Police Department
1122 M. D. Anderson Blvd.
795-0000

The purpose of the Medical Center police department is to suppress crime in the center. Officers patrol and handle problems outside buildings and enter facilities only on request of building security personnel. In June 1982, the department was certified as a police agency with all rights and authority of a certified police department.

Note: Car problems are under the jurisdiction of the Parking Department (see p. 117), rather than Medical Center police. The center has one truck, which can help with battery jumps. If a car needs towing, it is suggested that visitors call a wrecker.

The Medical Center contracts with a wrecker service to handle illegally parked cars (in wrong space, with improper or not current parking decals, those with previous tickets). Tickets are recorded on microfiche for ready reference. Violators are towed to the remote Brown Lot. If a car cannot be towed, it is chained in place.

University of Texas Police
7777 Knight Rd. (77054)
792-2890
Emergency: 792-HELP (4357)

The University of Texas Police Department has more than 150 guards and commissioned police officers. The department has its own academy in Austin (60 college hours are required).

The UT police ensure protection of life and property for employees and visitors to UT Health Science Center and Cancer Center facilities. Officers provide security inside and outside UT institutions in the Medical Center.

There are eight highly visible orange emergency phones outside UT buildings throughout the center. Most are near parking areas:
1. Near parking lot of Houston Main Building
2. Near Graduate School of Biomedical Sciences
3. South side of School of Public Health
4. East side of School of Public Health
5. West side of Dental Branch
6. West side of Speech and Hearing Institute
7. West side of John Freeman Building (UT Medical School)
8. East side of UT Medical School

The UT Police Department offers:
1. Escorts for visitors, employees, and patients to their cars after dark
2. Van rides for employees on night shifts to and from parking lots
3. Help with car starts
4. Calls to a service station or wrecker

10

WASHINGTON

MEMORIAL DRIVE

ALLEN   PARKWAY

TO
HOUSTON
INTER-
CONTINENTAL
AIRPORT

N

GREYHOUND
BUS
TERMINAL

COMMERCE

HARRISBURG

TRAILWAYS
BUS TERMINAL

59

TEXAS

WESTHEIMER

MAIN

KIRBY DRIVE

SHEPHERD

MONTROSE

45

TO
WILLIAM P. H
AIRPORT

59

ELGIN

TEXAS
MEDICAL
CENTER
MAIN
CAMPUS

SO. MAIN

HERMANN

288

W. LELAND
ANDERSON
CAMPUS

RICE
UNIVERSITY

FANNIN

OUTER

BELT

CALHOUN

TEXAS
MEDICAL
CENTER
AIRPORT
TERMINAL

HOLCOMBE

MAC GREGOR   WAY

ALT 90

OLD SPANISH   TRAIL

BRAESWOOD

CAMBRIDGE

ALMEDA DRIVE

VETERANS
ADMINIS-
TRATION
MEDICAL
CENTER

CULLEN BLVD

ASTRODOME

KIRBY DRIVE

FANNIN

SOUTH
EXTENSION
LOT
VISITOR
PARKING
288

610

TRANSPORTATION

Not all roads in Houston lead to the Texas Medical Center. Enough do, however, so that getting there from any place in Harris County is relatively easy. Here is a breakdown of available transportation and a few ideas for reaching the center from key locations.

FROM OUT OF TOWN
Automobile
While not directly beside a freeway, the Medical Center is accessible from every major route into Houston. Entering arteries lead downtown. Our map shows Fannin Street (which runs north-south and is one-way south in the central business district) south to the main site.

Intercity Buses
Trailways Bus System
2121 Main St.
759-6500

Greyhound Bus Lines
1410 Texas Ave.
222-1161

FROM AIRPORTS
Two major airports serve Houston. Hobby is approximately 10 miles from downtown, while Intercontinental is almost 30 miles north of the city.

Houston Intercontinental Airport
J. F. Kennedy Blvd. (between I-45 [North Fwy.] and U.S. 59 [Eastex Fwy.])

William P. Hobby Airport
Airport Blvd. (off I-45 South [Gulf Fwy.])

Texas Bus Lines Airport Express
Texas Medical Center Airport Terminal
2151 Holcombe Blvd.
664-3181

Hobby Airport Limousine Service, Inc.
Texas Medical Center Airport Terminal
2151 Holcombe Blvd.
644-8359

From both Hobby Airport and Houston Intercontinental, there is regular bus service to terminals around the city as well as limousine service to hotels. The Holcombe terminal has scheduled buses from both airports and is the station closest to the Medical Center. From the terminal, one can walk or take a cab or METRO bus to the center, only a few blocks away.

FROM TOWN
METRO (Metropolitan Transit Authority)
Texas Medical Center METRO Ride Store
Garage #2 (1155 Holcombe Blvd. at Bertner Ave.)
796-2969

METRO offers bus service to the Medical Center on many routes from downtown and other parts of the city. Buses display route numbers. Since routes change from time to time, call 635-4000 for up-to-date information and questions about your specific pickup point or destination.

There are several types of bus service: LOCAL makes frequent stops; LIMITED LOCAL eliminates some stops; EXPRESS runs nonstop most of its route; and PARK & RIDE originates from a designated parking lot and makes no stops until its primary destination. METROLift provides curb-to-curb transportation for physically or mentally handicapped persons for $1.00. Prior arrangements must be made by calling 225-0119.

Local and limited service costs 60¢; express service is 85¢; Park & Ride requires tickets, which must be purchased at METRO ticket outlets. Tickets are not sold at Park & Ride lots and cost varies with distance.

Tokens and monthly passes are available at METRO's Customer Service Center (1706 Milam, 7:30 AM to 5:00 PM, Monday through Friday, 658-0854), as well as ticket outlets throughout the region, or at the Medical Center Ride Store (9:30 AM to 12:00 PM and 1:00 PM to 4:00 PM, Monday through Friday, 796-2969). Medical Center employees receive a 10 percent discount on ticket books.

METRO provides free circulating routes at the Medical Center. Regular routes from outside connect to METRO's three circulating routes (see Getting Around in Texas Medical Center, p. 116).

Taxis

Yellow Cab	236-1111
Liberty Cab	695-6700
Sky-Jack's Cab Company	523-6080
United Taxicab Company	699-0000

Because Houston has fewer cabs per person than most metropolitan areas and because of the geographic size of the area, it is hard to "flag" a ride. Taxis are acquired by calling in to the radio dispatchers and asking for a cab at a specific location at a specific time. Drivers are punctual and reliable about showing up, but during peak hours and on rainy days you may have to wait. Cab rates are reasonable and most operators will honor a prearranged pickup time. United Taxicab will schedule vans for wheelchair pickup with 24-hour notice.

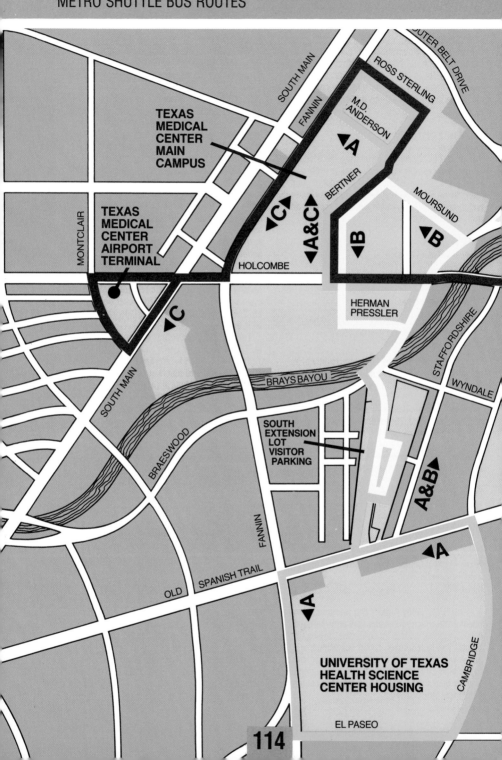

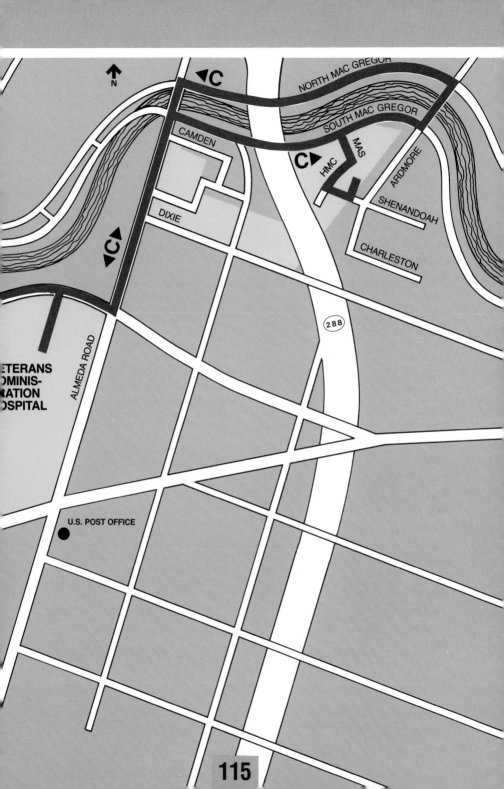

For Disabled

The Houston Center for Independent Living (795-4252) offers information and referrals to agencies that provide transportation and other services for disabled persons.

Hospital social workers can arrange free transportation through the Red Cross (526-8300) for individuals not qualified for other programs.

From Hotels/Motels

Many hotels in the vicinity of Texas Medical Center have regular courtesy guest transportation from their front door to any spot inside the center. Most places offering this service do not charge, but it is always nice to tip the driver. Be sure to ask about this service before checking into a hotel. The cost of three trips a day can mount up, whether you pay for cab rides or for parking. The free Medical Center circulator bus service includes a few nearby hotels.

EMERGENCY TRANSPORTATION

Houston Ambulance
911 or 222-3434

Emergency ambulances, complete with paramedics, are operated by the Houston Fire Department.

The Greater Harris County Emergency Network Organization offers a 911 emergency number to summon any kind of help (ambulance, police, fire).

Life Flight is a helicopter ambulance from Hermann Hospital for emergencies where ground transportation might not be available or would take too long. Choppers are fully equipped with life support systems, and the airborne team consists of a doctor and a nurse. Life Flight must be summoned by police, fire fighters, doctors, or hospital personnel.

GETTING AROUND IN TEXAS MEDICAL CENTER

METRO Ride Store
Garage #2 (1155 Holcombe Blvd. at Bertner Ave.) 796-2969; METRO route and schedule information: 635-4000
Other numbers:
Parking Department (1522 Braeswood) 797-9445
  Remote long-term (South Extension Lot) parking, vehicle towing, tickets, etc.
Parking Permit Office (Garage #2   790-9022
  Temporary handicapped display cards, employee parking permits, permits for ministers, general questions.
Texas Medical Center Police   795-0000
  Regarding security.
  Transportation around the center is a free service provided by Texas Medical Center.

METRO offers three circulator routes. Each route is marked with a letter and a color. Colored flags make buses easy to identify. Routes are listed on bus stop signs.

ROUTE A: Green flags
M–F, 4:30 AM–1:00 AM; Su, 7:00 PM to 1:00 AM
Every 4 minutes during peak hours (6:00 AM to 8:30 AM and 2:00 PM to 6:00 PM); every 20 minutes during regular hours. Combined with Route B, service provided every 2 minutes in peak times; every 10 minutes at other times.

Service to and from:
Remote long-term (South Extension Lot) parking
UTHSCH School of Public Health
M. D. Anderson Hospital and Tumor Institute
St. Luke's Episcopal Hospital
Texas Children's Hospital
Methodist Hospital
Texas Woman's University—Houston Center
Baylor College of Medicine
Jesse H. Jones Library Building
UTHSCH Medical School
Hermann Hospital
UT Apartments (student housing) on selected trips

ROUTE B: Gold flags
M–F, 6:00 AM–8:00 PM
Every 4 minutes during peak hours (6:00 AM to 8:30 AM and 2:00 PM to 6:00 PM); every 20 minutes during regular hours. Combined with Route A, service provided every 2 minutes in peak times; every 10 minutes at other times.

Service to and from:
Remote long-term (South Extension Lot) parking
City of Houston Department of Health and Human Services
UT Mental Sciences Institute
Institute for Rehabilitation and Research
UTHSCH Dental Branch
Baylor College of Medicine
Texas Woman's University—Houston Center
Methodist Hospital
St. Luke's Episcopal Hospital
M. D. Anderson Hospital and Tumor Institute
UTHSCH School of Public Health

ROUTE C: Maroon flags
M–F, 6:00 AM to 6:00 PM
Operates every 20 minutes.

Service to and from:
Leland Anderson Campus:
  High School for Health Professions

Renilda Hilkemeyer Child Care Center
Houston Community College System Health
   Careers Education Division
Harris County Psychiatric Center
St. Anthony Center
New Age Hospice of Houston
Veterans Administration Medical Center
Texas Medical Center and UT Housing on
   Holcombe
M. D. Anderson Hospital and Tumor Institute
St. Luke's Episcopal Hospital
Texas Children's Hospital
Methodist Hospital
Baylor College of Medicine
Texas Woman's University—Houston Center
Jesse H. Jones Library Building
Scurlock Tower
Marriott Hotel
Holiday Inn
Rodeway Towers
Shamrock Hilton Hotel
Fannin/Holcombe Building
Ben Taub General Hospital
UTHSCH Medical School
Prairie View A&M University College·of Nursing

ROUTE D: Blue flags
M–F, 6:00 AM–12:00 PM
This additional route, similar to Route C, has re-
cently been added.

PARKING
Parking Department
1522 Braeswood, north entrance to South Extension Lot
797-9445
   Visitors and patients may park in Medical Center garages or designated visitor lots (see map).
Hourly rates are standard throughout the center,
with the exception of lots not owned by the center:
next to Hermann Hospital (at Fannin Street and
Outer Belt), where rates are quite high; at Ben
Taub, where rates are reasonable; and at the City
of Houston Department of Health and Human Services, where limited parking for visitors to the
Health Department is free.
   Maximum daily parking is $7.00. In-and-out
privileges are allowed if you save your parking re-
ceipt for same day return. Additional fees will ac-
cumulate, but will total no more than the maximum amount.
   The satellite South Extension Lot (off Braeswood Boulevard, near Wyndale) is recommended
for those who will be at the Medical Center for
extended periods of time and want the most eco-
nomical parking. Free METRO service is provided
from the South Extension Lot to institutions inside

the center. Maximum daily satellite parking to-
tals $1.05.
   Short-term parking is available at meters in a
few locations. Quarters are needed for meters.
   A temporary handicapped display card for patients or visitors whose mobility is temporarily
impaired may be obtained at the Parking Permit
Office (Garage #2, 790-9022). Cars displaying
permits may park legally in "handicapped only"
designated places.

TUNNELS AND SKYWALKS
Movement inside the Medical Center, especially on
hot or rainy days, can be made much easier by using the maze of underground tunnels and aboveground skywalks.
   The biggest problem is discovering how to enter
the system. The list below is a guide. Employees
and frequent visitors make use of these walkways,
so don't hesitate to ask directions.

Garage #1 to St. Luke's Episcopal Hospital, Texas
Children's Hospital, and Texas Heart Institute
   Enter tunnel from Garage #1's lower level "G".
It goes to the hospitals' "LL" (lower level). The
door to the garage is locked 9:30 PM to 6:00 AM.

Garage #1 to Methodist Hospital
   Enter tunnel from Garage #1's lower level "G"
Signs mark the tunnel to Methodist Hospital's
lower level. An elevator from the lower level takes
passengers to Methodist's ground floor, across
from the cafeteria.

St. Luke's Episcopal Hospital, Texas Children's
Hospital, and Texas Heart Institute to Methodist
Hospital
   The same tunnel that connects Garage #1 to St.
Luke's, Texas Children's, and Texas Heart Institute
in one direction and to Methodist Hospital in the
other direction connects these hospitals together.
It goes from St. Luke's and Texas Children's "LL"
to Methodist's lower level.

Methodist Hospital to Scurlock Tower (above Fan-
nin Street) to Fondren Orthopedic Center, Brown
Cardiovascular Research Center, and Alkek Tower
to Neurosensory Center
   The buildings are all part of the Methodist Hospital complex and are connected by skywalks and
tunnels. A skywalk goes from Methodist Hospital's
second floor, over Fannin Street, to Scurlock
Tower. This walkway also continues on to Fondren-
Brown buildings and the Neurosensory Center.
   .One can enter a tunnel in the Neurosensory
Center at the Jones Patient Tower on "G" floor at
the lobby. It goes to Fondren-Brown buildings and

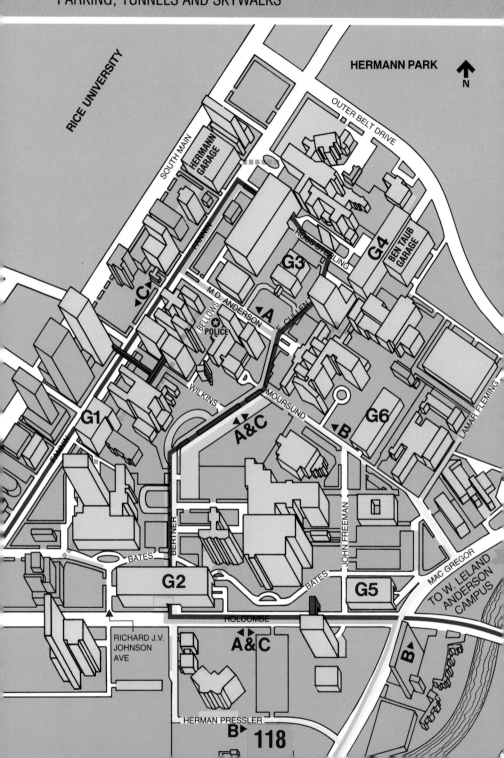

Alkek Tower and splits to go around the perimeter of the main Methodist Hospital building. At the split, one way leads to St. Luke's Hospital (which includes Texas Children's Hospital and Texas Heart Institute); the other way also leads to St. Luke's Hospital, by way of Garage #1.

M. D. Anderson Hospital and Tumor Institute to Garage #2
An underground tunnel goes from M. D. Anderson's Lutheran Pavilion to Garage #2, but it is opened only when it rains for employees to reach their cars.

M. D. Anderson Hospital and Tumor Institute's housing complex to main campus.
An elevated walkway over Holcombe Boulevard connects the UT Cancer Center's complex to the Medical Center main campus.

Hermann Hospital to Hermann Professional Building (under Fannin Street)
A rounded, greenly lit, space-age tunnel goes under Fannin Street from Hermann Hospital's Jones Pavilion "SB" (subbasement) level to Hermann Professional Building's Garage (which is connected to Hermann Professional Building).

Hermann Hospital to Shriners Hospital for Crippled Children
This tunnel is traveled only by those who have a need to use it. It goes from Hermann Hospital's Jones Pavilion "G" (ground) level (near the mail room) to Shriners Hospital's "B" level (near the pool). A door at the Shriners Hospital end is kept locked.

Hermann Hospital to University of Texas Medical School (across Ross Sterling Avenue at Entrance #1)
UT Medical School's nine-story building bridges Ross Sterling Avenue and forms a continuous complex with Hermann Hospital. On all floors above ground level, one can cross over Ross Sterling Avenue from Hermann Hospital to the UT Medical School.
At street level, there is a covered breezeway from the UT Medical School's cafeteria (which is on the Hermann Hospital side of the street) across Ross Sterling Avenue to the UT Medical School building.
The UT Medical School is connected to the UT Freeman Building (at M. D. Anderson Boulevard). It is therefore possible to go by tunnel from the Freeman Building to Hermann Hospital, Hermann Professional Building, and Shriners Hospital.

Laurence Favrot Hall to Texas Woman's University Dorm
One can travel from Favrot Hall to TWU's dorm inside through the basement.

Baylor College of Medicine to Ben Taub General Hospital
An underground tunnel goes from Baylor College of Medicine's main building to its DeBakey Building. The walkway splits and one leg leads to Ben Taub. It is therefore possible to go from Baylor to Ben Taub, Baylor to DeBakey, Ben Taub to DeBakey, and Ben Taub to Baylor.
One can go from Baylor's main building to the DeBakey Building on the first floor without using the tunnel.

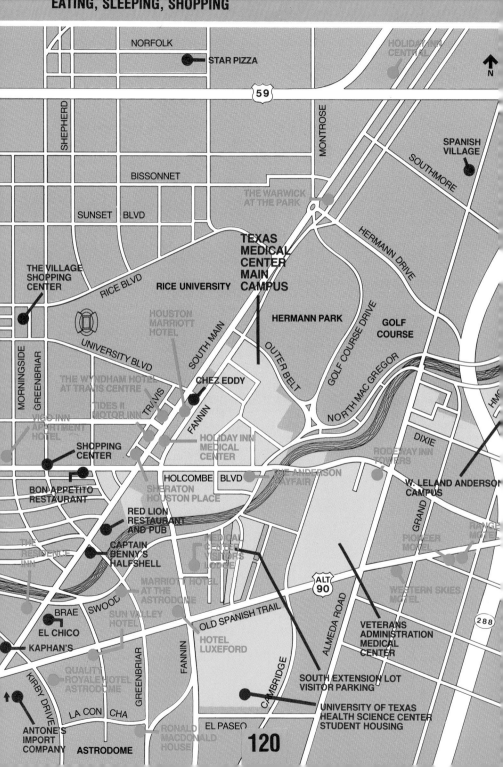

NORFOLK

STAR PIZZA

HOLIDAY INN
CENTRAL

59

SHEPHERD

MONTROSE

SPANISH
VILLAGE

SOUTHMORE

BISSONNET

THE WARWICK
AT THE PARK

HERMANN DRIVE

SUNSET BLVD

TEXAS
MEDICAL
CENTER
MAIN
CAMPUS

THE VILLAGE
SHOPPING
CENTER

RICE BLVD

RICE UNIVERSITY

HERMANN PARK

GOLF
COURSE

GOLF COURSE DRIVE

MORNINGSIDE

GREENBRIAR

UNIVERSITY BLVD

HOUSTON
MARRIOTT
HOTEL

SOUTH MAIN

OUTER BELT

NORTH MAC GREGOR

HMC

THE WYNDHAM HOTEL
AT TRAVIS CENTRE

TIDES II
MOTOR INN

CHEZ EDDY

TRAVIS

FANNIN

DIXIE

VGO INN
APARTMENT
HOTEL

SHOPPING
CENTER

HOLIDAY INN
MEDICAL
CENTER

RODEWAY INN
TOWERS

W. LELAND ANDERSON
CAMPUS

BON APPETITO
RESTAURANT

HOLCOMBE BLVD

THE ANDERSON
MAYFAIR

GRAND

SHERATON
HOUSTON PLACE

RANGE
MOTEL

RED LION
RESTAURANT
AND PUB

MEDICAL
CENTER
VISITORS
LODGE

PIONEER
MOTEL

THE
RESIDENCE
INN

CAPTAIN
BENNY'S
HALFSHELL

ALT
90

WESTERN SKIES
MOTEL

MARRIOTT HOTEL
AT THE
ASTRODOME

SWOOD

BRAE

EL CHICO

SUN VALLEY
HOTEL

OLD SPANISH TRAIL

ALMEDA ROAD

288

VETERANS
ADMINISTRATION
MEDICAL
CENTER

KAPHAN'S

FANNIN

HOTEL
LUXEFORD

CAMBRIDGE

KIRBY DRIVE

QUALITY
ROYALE HOTEL
ASTRODOME

GREENBRIAR

SOUTH EXTENSION LOT
VISITOR PARKING

LA CON CHA

ANTONE'S
IMPORT
COMPANY

ASTRODOME

RONALD
MACDONALD
HOUSE

EL PASEO

120

UNIVERSITY OF TEXAS
HEALTH SCIENCE CENTER
STUDENT HOUSING

N

EATING PLACES

As in any large city, eating places run the gamut from six stools along a counter to elegance almost to the point of sinfulness. Prices for meals follow the same diversity. Another problem with restaurants lies in a propensity to be open today and gone tomorrow. Any list is frequently outdated, but a quick count shows over one hundred reputable places to eat within about a three-mile radius of the Medical Center, in addition to the hotels in the area, which all have dining facilities.

Be sure to call any restaurant you select to determine hours, days closed, and credit card information. Reservations are best in the places that accept them. Better to ask in advance than have to wait after you arrive.

The Yellow Pages of the telephone book list hundreds of additional places to dine or snack. In general, any address on South Main Street, Holcombe Boulevard, Montrose Boulevard, or Kirby Drive will be reasonably close to the Medical Center.

In alphabetical order, here's a listing of several places that have been in business for some years, are popular with Medical Center staffers, and are frequently mentioned in response to questions about where to eat.

Antone's Import Company
7807 Kirby
666-4191

A delicatessen inside an imported-food grocery store. Seating is limited; sandwiches, especially "Poor Boys," are great and can be had "to go." Open for breakfast, lunch, and dinner. Beer and wine. *Inexpensive.*

Bon Apetito Restaurant
2231 Holcombe Blvd.
665-4601

A good Italian restaurant in an old home. Open for lunch and dinner. Full bar service. *Moderate.*

Brennan's Houston
3300 Smith St.
522-9711

An exceptional dining establishment. Creole and American cuisine. Lunch and dinner. Full bar service. *Moderate to expensive.*

Captain Benny's Half Shell
7409 South Main St.
795-9051

A quirky seafood restaurant in the hull of an old shrimp boat. Oysters on the half shell, gumbo, boiled shrimp, etc. Lunch and dinner. Beer and wine. *Inexpensive to moderate.*

Chez Eddy
6560 Fannin St.
4th Floor, Scurlock Tower
790-6474

Healthy (no salt or cream) gourmet food. Lunch and dinner. Beer and wine. *Moderate to expensive.*

El Chico International
7707 South Main St.
797-9311

Mexican food in an elegant setting. Lunch and dinner. Full bar service. *Inexpensive to moderate.*

Goode Company Barbeque
5109 Kirby Dr.
522-2530

Texas barbeque with all the trimmings. Lunch and dinner. Beer and wine. *Inexpensive to moderate.*

Kaphan's
7900 South Main St. (at Kirby)
668-0491

A long-established, well-respected seafood and steak house. Lunch and dinner. Full bar service. *Moderate.*

Red Lion Restaurant and Pub
7315 South Main St.
795-5000

Roast beef and other English specialties in an unusual setting. Dinner nightly; lunch, Monday through Friday. Full bar service. *Moderate to expensive.*

Spanish Village
4720 Almeda Rd.
523-1727

Tex-Mex cooking, some say the best in Texas, in a curiously funky atmosphere and the feeling that this place has been here a while. It has. Lunch and dinner. Full bar service. *Inexpensive to moderate.*

Star Pizza
2111 Norfolk St.
523-0800

Sandwiches, salads, and pizza that have become standard fare with many who work in the Medical Center. Delivers in the evenings. Lunch and dinner. Beer and wine. *Inexpensive.*

PLACES TO STAY

A great many places near the Medical Center are designed to accommodate individuals, couples, or entire families for stays ranging from a single night to weeks at a time. Prices change rapidly, and there are many variables from one motel or hotel to another; therefore, in place of actual dollars, a general range of costs is indicated in our list. At times, and under certain conditions, special rates for those visiting the center may be in effect. When calling for reservations, inquire about a Medical Center rate.

In selecting lodging, be sure to get the whole picture. An "inexpensive" room might end up costing as much or more than a "moderate" accommodation if the hotel offering the "moderate" rate also provides free transportation door to door from the hotel to your destination in the Medical Center. Another point to consider is nearness to the center. Hotels marked • are closer than those not marked. Finally, such extras as 30-plus channel TV, late-hour room service, or, if you don't have a car in Houston, availability of taxis might be important. Consider the entire package before making a decision.

These listings are merely given as a guide. They should not be considered an endorsement of any kind.

HOTEL/MOTEL • *Near Texas Medical Center*	PRICE RANGE	MEDICAL CENTER TRANSPORTATION PROVIDED
• Alamo Plaza Motel 4343 Old Spanish Tr. (77021) 747-6900	Inexpensive	No
Almost Heaven Camp Grounds 4202 Del Bello Rd. Out Highway 288, off County Road 58 Manvel, TX (77578) 489-8561	Inexpensive	No
• The Anderson Mayfair (The University of Texas at Houston) 1600 Holcombe Blvd. (77030) 790-1600	Moderate	Yes
• Astro Village Hotel and Lodge 2350 South Loop West (Loop 610 at Kirby) (77054) 748-3221	Moderate	Yes
Bed and Breakfast Society of Houston 921 Heights Blvd. (77008) 868-4654 Placement in private homes	Inexpensive	No
Bestway Motor Inn 4115 Gulf Freeway (77023) 225-0011	Inexpensive	No
• Brompton Court Apartments 7510 Brompton Blvd. (at North Braeswood) (77025) 666-4138 Furnished; 30-day minimum	Moderate	Yes
• Chief Motel 9000 South Main St. (77025) 666-4151	Inexpensive	Yes

122

HOTEL/MOTEL • *Near Texas Medical Center*	PRICE RANGE	MEDICAL CENTER TRANSPORTATION PROVIDED
• Crestwood Motel 9001 South Main St. (77025) 667-5691	Inexpensive	No
• The Grant Motor Inn 8200 South Main St. (77025) 668-8000	Inexpensive	Yes
Holiday House Motel 10319 South Main St. (77025) 664-3481	Inexpensive	No
• Holiday Inn—Astro Village 8500 Kirby Dr. (at Loop 610) (77054) 799-1050	Moderate	Yes
Holiday Inn—Central 4640 Main St. (77002) 526-2811	Moderate	Yes
• Holiday Inn—Medical Center 6701 South Main St. (77030) 797-1110	Moderate	Yes
Holiday Inn—Near Greenway Plaza 2712 Southwest Freeway (77098) 523-8448	First class	Yes
• Hotel Luxeford 1400 Old Spanish Tr. (77054) 796-1000 All suites	Moderate	Yes
Houston Campgrounds 710 State Highway 6 South (1/2 mile south of I-10) (77079) 493-2391	Inexpensive	No
• Houston Marriott Hotel—Medical Center 6580 Fannin St. (77030) 796-0080	First class	Yes
• Houston Villa Motor Hotel 9604 South Main St. (77025) 666-1411	Inexpensive	No
Hyatt Regency Houston 1200 Louisiana St. (77002) 654-1234	First class	Yes
La Quinta Motor Inn—Greenway 4015 Southwest Freeway (77027) 623-4750	Moderate	No

HOTEL/MOTEL • Near Texas Medical Center	PRICE RANGE	MEDICAL CENTER TRANSPORTATION PROVIDED
• Marriott Hotel at the Astrodome 2100 South Braeswood Blvd. (at Greenbriar) (77030) 797-9000	First class	Yes
• Medical Center Visitors Lodge 1025 Swanson St. (77030) 790-1617 Suites only; daily or monthly rental	Inexpensive	Yes
Mitchell Inn 10015 South Main St. (77025) 667-9173	Inexpensive	No
• Old South Trailer Park 8803 South Main St. (77025) 665-9344	Inexpensive	No
• Pine Shadows Travel Trailer Park and Campground 8080 South Main St. (77025) 664-4371	Inexpensive	No
• Pioneer Motel 2902 Old Spanish Tr. (77054) 747-7021	Inexpensive	No
Quality Inn—Greenway Plaza 4020 Southwest Freeway (77027) 623-4720	Inexpensive	Yes
• Quality Royale Hotel—Astrodome 8111 Kirby Dr. (77054) 790-1900	First class	Yes
Ramada Greenway Plaza Hotel 2929 Southwest Freeway (77098) 528-6161	Moderate	Yes
• Ranger Motel 2916 Old Spanish Tr. (77054) 747-3300	Inexpensive	Yes
• Regal 8 8500 South Main St. (77025) 666-4971	Inexpensive	Yes
• The Residence Inn—Astrodome 7710 South Main St. (at Braeswood) (77030) 660-7993 All furnished suites	Moderate	Yes
Rodeway #141 3135 Southwest Freeway (77098) 526-1071	Moderate	No

HOTEL/MOTEL • Near Texas Medical Center	PRICE RANGE	MEDICAL CENTER TRANSPORTATION PROVIDED
• Rodeway Inn—Towers 2130 Holcombe Blvd. (77030) 666-1461	Moderate	Yes
• Ronald McDonald House 1550 La Concha Ln. (77054) 797-0332	Free	Yes

Supported by area corporations and organizations, provides a home-like environment for families of children undergoing long-term hospital stays. For details, contact Texas Children's Hospital, Social Service 791-2149.

• Sahara Main Motel and RV Park 9051 South Main St. (77025) 661-8822	Inexpensive	No
• Sheraton Houston Place Hotel at the Medical Center 6800 South Main St. (77030) 528-7744	Moderate	Yes
South Houston Trailer Park 615 South Allen Genoa Rd. (77017) 943-3725	Inexpensive	No
• South Main Trailer Village 10100 South Main St. (77025) 667-0120	Inexpensive	No
Stouffer's Greenway Plaza Hotel 6 Greenway Plaza East (77046) 629-1200	First class	Yes
• Sun Valley Hotel 1310 Old Spanish Tr. (77054) 790-1166	Inexpensive	Yes
• Surrey House Motor Hotel 8330 South Main St. (77025) 667-9261	Inexpensive	Yes
• Texian Inn—Astrodome 9911 Buffalo Speedway (at Loop 610) (77054) 668-8082	Moderate	Yes
• Tides II Motor Inn 6700 South Main St. (77030) 522-2811	Inexpensive	Yes
• Travelodge—Astrodome 8700 South Main St. (77025) 666-0346	Moderate	Yes
• Vigo Inn Apartment Hotel 6712 Morningside Dr. (77030) 663-6200	Moderate	Yes

HOTEL/MOTEL • *Near Texas Medical Center*	PRICE RANGE	MEDICAL CENTER TRANSPORTATION PROVIDED
Viscount Hotel of Houston 2828 Southwest Freeway (77098) 526-4571	Moderate	Yes
• The Warwick at the Park 5701 Main St. (77251) 526-1991	Deluxe	Yes
• Western Skies Motel 2806 Old Spanish Tr. (77054) 747-2300	Inexpensive	No
• White House Motor Hotel 9300 South Main St. (77025) 666-2261	Moderate	Yes
• The Wyndham Hotel at Travis Centre 6633 Travis St. (at Southgate) (77030) 524-6633	Deluxe	Yes

NEARBY SHOPPING CENTERS

The University Village
Closest large shopping area to the Medical Center; between Kirby Drive and Greenbriar, concentrated around Rice Boulevard and Rice University; a variety of stores, shops, businesses, and restaurants.

Greenbriar at Holcombe
Small center minutes from the Medical Center; grocery, cleaners, drugstore, eating places, shops.

Meyerland Plaza
West Loop 610, Beechnut exit; large regional shopping center a convenient driving distance from the Medical Center; many stores, restaurants, movie theaters.

Weslayan Plaza
Weslayan at Bissonnet; grocery, drugstore, stores, shops, eating places.

What can you do when you have an hour and a half to wait? You can sit in a reception area and read old magazines or you can explore the Texas Medical Center.

Libraries, gift shops, and bookstores are scattered throughout the center, but there are even more exciting things to see. Take a walking tour of the Medical Center to get an overall picture of this enormous complex. Take the children along. The buildings mentioned below are inside the main campus or can be reached by tunnel or skywalk.

HERMANN HOSPITAL

Begin at Hermann Hospital, which is known as the Life Flight Hospital. Three Life Flight helicopters, emergency air ambulances, are based at the John Dunn Heliport (donated by John S. Dunn). The hospital has a major emergency center.

Hermann opened in 1925. The original hospital building faces Hermann Park and has a beautiful tiled lobby. An art collection is on permanent display in Hermann's Eye Center.

From Hermann Hospital (Jones Pavilion "SB" level), it is possible to take a tunnel under Fannin Street to the Hermann Professional Building Garage. The tunnel is rather like a science fiction set. There are shops and eating places in the Hermann Professional Building.

Hermann is the primary teaching hospital for the University of Texas Medical School, to which it is joined (over Ross Sterling Avenue). Visit UT Medical School's cafeteria on the Hermann Hospital side of Ross Sterling Avenue near entrance #1. Pass by a travel agency on your way.

Also of interest is the Mirtha G. Dunn Interfaith Chapel (given by Mr. Dunn in memory of his wife) in front of the Robertson Pavilion. Its distinctive triangular shape is reminiscent of the Air Force Academy chapel's "praying hands" design. The triangular stained-glass windows were designed by San Antonio artist Cecil Long Casbier. Each piece of glass was hand-chipped, so that no two pieces are alike. They were placed at random in the copper frames to give unusual light-scattering patterns. Inside the chapel is a 35-foot wool tapestry, with more than 4 million hand-tied knots. It was designed by Matt Kahn and weighs more than six hundred pounds. The altar is made of Alabama marble on a brass base. The electronic organ was built especially for this chapel (and donated by Mr. and Mrs. Neill Amsler, Jr., in memory of their children).

SHRINERS HOSPITAL FOR CRIPPLED CHILDREN

Shriners Hospital is next door to Hermann Hospital and uses Hermann's food service facilities. This building was opened in 1951 and is supported by Shriners. No charge is made to patients by the hospital. Doctors donate their services as well. Children, age 18 and under, are treated more as family than as patients at Shriners.

Facts about the fountain in front of the hospital are few. This gift from Mr. and Mrs. S. P. Martell came from Europe and was installed in its present location about 1953.

BEN TAUB GENERAL HOSPITAL

Ben Taub is the Harris County Hospital District's main hospital. It provides medical care for indigent residents of Harris County and is known as one of the two major emergency centers in Houston (Hermann Hospital is the other). The building, opened in 1963, has recently undergone some much needed renovations. This building will be used for office space when the new hospital is completed.

Ben Taub is a teaching facility for Baylor College of Medicine. The two buildings are connected by tunnel.

BAYLOR COLLEGE OF MEDICINE

Baylor, the only private medical school in the Southwest, moved into the Cullen Building in 1947. Since that time, it has added a ten-story research tower.

Students can enter M.D. and Ph.D. programs and receive training at Ben Taub (and other Harris County Hospital District facilities), Methodist Hospital, St. Luke's and Texas Children's hospitals, Institute for Rehabilitation and Research, and Veterans Administration Medical Center.

In front of the old Cullen Building is the Alkek Fountain, named in honor of Albert B. Alkek, an oilman, rancher, conservationist, and long-time supporter of Baylor. In front of the Michael E. De-Bakey Center for Biomedical Education and Research is an interesting steel sculpture, by Mark di Suvero, titled *Pranath Yama*, a Hindu phrase that concerns the cycle of life and death. Inside Baylor College of Medicine is an untitled fresco by David Novros.

THE INSTITUTE FOR REHABILITATION AND RESEARCH (TIRR)

The TIRR building adjoins the University of Texas Speech and Hearing Institute, behind Baylor College of Medicine. TIRR had its beginning as a rehabilitation center for polio victims in an old house in the Montrose area. Today it has become a treatment and research center for rehabilitation for many physical handicaps. Programs are designed to give a patient maximum independence in a satisfying and fulfilling life style.

Prometheus Unbound, the statue at TIRR's west

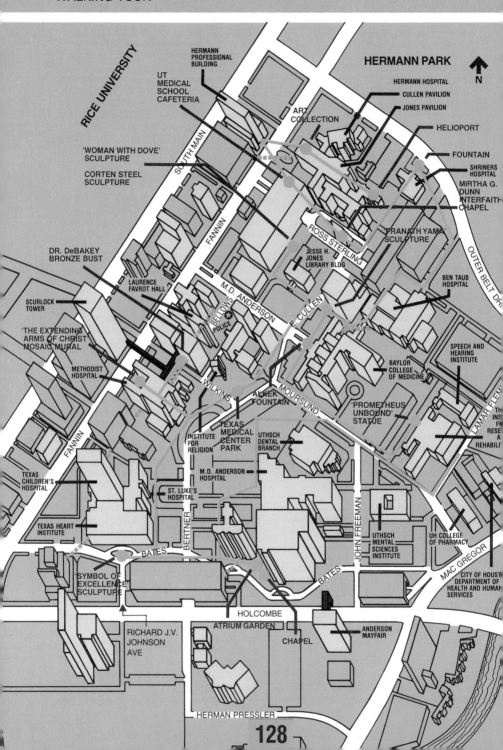

RICE UNIVERSITY

HERMANN
PROFESSIONAL
BUILDING

UT
MEDICAL
SCHOOL
CAFETERIA

HERMANN PARK

N

ART
COLLECTION

HERMANN HOSPITAL

CULLEN PAVILION

JONES PAVILION

HELIOPORT

SOUTH MAIN

'WOMAN WITH DOVE'
SCULPTURE

CORTEN STEEL
SCULPTURE

FOUNTAIN

SHRINERS
HOSPITAL

MIRTHA G.
DUNN
INTERFAITH
CHAPEL

FANNIN

ROSS STERLING

'PRANATH YAMA'
SCULPTURE

DR. DeBAKEY
BRONZE BUST

JESSE H.
JONES
LIBRARY BLDG

OUTER BELT DR.

LAURENCE
FAVROT HALL

M.D. ANDERSON

BEN TAUB
HOSPITAL

SCURLOCK
TOWER

BELLOWS
POLICE

E. CULLEN

'THE EXTENDING
ARMS OF CHRIST'
MOSAIC MURAL

SPEECH AND
HEARING
INSTITUTE

METHODIST
HOSPITAL

BAYLOR
COLLEGE
OF MEDICINE

WILKINS

MOURSUND

ALKEK
FOUNTAIN

FANNIN

INSTITUTE
FOR
RELIGION

TEXAS
MEDICAL
CENTER
PARK

UTHSCH
DENTAL
BRANCH

'PROMETHEUS
UNBOUND'
STATUE

LAMAR FLEM

TH
INS
F
RESE
A
REHABILI

TEXAS
CHILDREN'S
HOSPITAL

M.D. ANDERSON
HOSPITAL

UH COLLEGE
OF PHARMACY

ST. LUKE'S
HOSPITAL

BERTNER

JOHN FREEMAN

TEXAS HEART
INSTITUTE

UTHSCH
MENTAL
SCIENCES
INSTITUTE

MAC GREGOR

BATES

CITY OF HOUS
DEPARTMENT OF
HEALTH AND HUMAN
SERVICES

'SYMBOL OF
EXCELLENCE'
SCULPTURE

BATES

RICHARD J.V.
JOHNSON
AVE

HOLCOMBE

ATRIUM GARDEN

CHAPEL

ANDERSON
MAYFAIR

HERMAN PRESSLER

entrance, symbolizes the freedom from shackles to be gained through rehabilitation.

UT SPEECH AND HEARING INSTITUTE
The Speech and Hearing Institute is part of the University of Texas Health Science Center at Houston. There is help here for the communicatively handicapped. It is a center for research and graduate studies in the areas of speech, language, and hearing.

CITY OF HOUSTON DEPARTMENT OF HEALTH AND HUMAN SERVICES
Across Lamar Fleming Street is Houston's Department of Health and Human Services. Concerned with preventable disease control and health care problems of the community, the Medical Center location is known as "Central," because it has the administrative offices for the department.

UNIVERSITY OF HOUSTON COLLEGE OF PHARMACY
Separated from the Department of Health and Human Services by a grassy area is the University of Houston's branch at the Medical Center. The College of Pharmacy makes it possible for students to have contact with patients, physicians, allied health personnel, and working pharmacists. Its 24-hour Turner Drug Information Center gives drug information to the public and to medical professionals.

UT MENTAL SCIENCES INSTITUTE
Across Moursund Avenue from the UH College of Pharmacy and the Institute for Rehabilitation and Research is the UT Mental Sciences Institute, a psychiatric research facility, working in the areas of alcohol and drug abuse, aging, mental retardation, and many other facets of mental health.

M. D. ANDERSON HOSPITAL AND TUMOR INSTITUTE
The pink Georgian marble building across John Freeman Street is M. D. Anderson. This huge complex is part of the University of Texas System Cancer Center. While it shares facilities with the UT Health Science Center at Houston (in the old Prudential Building across Holcombe Boulevard), it is administered separately.

M. D. Anderson is probably the most people-oriented facility in the Medical Center. Explanatory signs are posted, information desks are staffed with helpful personnel, HELP! phones (for directions and information) are located in strategic areas, and printed literature is available (one newspaper details a 30-minute self-guided tour).

The Atrium Garden, a patio with tables, umbrellas, and chairs, is near the cafeteria, where patients and visitors may enjoy lunch or snacks. The chapel, with the Freeman-Dunn Sanctuary, seats one hundred in triangular sets of pews surrounding the central marble altar. Its stained-glass windows depict Holy Baptism, the Trinity, and Holy Communion. A tunnel connects M. D. Anderson's Lutheran Pavilion to Garage #2. It is opened for employees when it rains.

Also included in the UT System Cancer Center is the Rehabilitation Center (outlying), the Anderson Mayfair patient and family hotel (across Holcombe Boulevard), and a research center in Bastrop County. A skywalk joins the Anderson Mayfair complex with the Texas Medical Center campus, providing a safe crossing of Holcombe Boulevard. It seems as though more space is always being added to M. D. Anderson.

ST. LUKE'S EPISCOPAL HOSPITAL, TEXAS CHILDREN'S HOSPITAL, AND TEXAS HEART INSTITUTE
Don't miss the red granite heart sculpture at the Bates Street entrance to St. Luke's and Texas Children's hospitals and Texas Heart Institute. *Symbol of Excellence* was created by Theodore H. McKinney as an expression of gratitude for heart surgery performed on his daughter, and later himself.

St. Luke's Episcopal Hospital was founded in 1954 and Texas Children's Hospital opened that same year to offer special care to children. Because both St. Luke's and Texas Children's were deeply involved in cardiovascular medicine, the Texas Heart Institute was created in 1962. The Heart Institute is not a hospital but an institutional program for education, treatment, and research of cardiovascular diseases.

Several eating places (cafeteria, coffee shop, and canteen) are located in this complex. Also of interest are gift shops (Texas Children's gift shop is as much fun as a toy store) and the Cullen Memorial Chapel.

THE METHODIST HOSPITAL
Next door is Methodist Hospital. There are several ways to get there from St. Luke's and Texas Children's hospitals. You can go by tunnel from St. Luke's and Texas Children's lower level ("LL") to Garage #1 ("G" floor) to Methodist Hospital's lower level. However, if the day is nice, walk outside past Methodist's and St. Luke's laundry (it cleans linens and towels with chemicals instead of soap), which backs up to Garage #1. Next to it is Methodist's Emergency Center.

Walk up the semicircular drive to Methodist Hospital's main building. (Methodist takes in several buildings, listed below.) Inside, take the walkway to the Brown-Fondren-Alkek complex and the skywalk from Methodist (floor 2) to the Scurlock Tower, over Fannin Street. Enjoy the art along the way. Explore the shops, eating places, and businesses in the Scurlock Tower. If you want a gourmet French lunch (or dinner), visit Chez Eddy on the fourth floor of the Scurlock Tower. If time is limited, phone ahead for lunch-to-go service. The restaurant serves wine and beer.

Back across the skywalk (on the Medical Center side) over Fannin Street, you can continue to the Brown Cardiovascular Research Center, the Alkek Tower, and the Fondren Orthopedic Center. These buildings are connected to the Neurosensory Center. All are part of the Methodist Hospital complex. It is possible to go from Bates Street to M. D. Anderson Boulevard indoors.

Before you leave the Methodist Hospital main building, step outside the Fannin Street entrance to view the mosaic mural, *The Extending Arms of Christ*. It was designed by artist Bruce Hayes, constructed in Florence, Italy, of more than 1.5 million pieces of mosaic glass, and installed in 1963. Divided into three main sections, the mural suggests the importance of medicine and religion in our past and present. The focal point is the Christ figure superimposed upon the hospital's Wiess Memorial Chapel.

A bronze bust of Dr. DeBakey, sculpted by French artist Georges Muguet, stands at the Wilkins Avenue entrance to the Fondren and Brown buildings. In 1978, it was presented to Dr. De-Bakey by His Majesty King Leopold of Belgium and Her Royal Highness Princess Lilian.

THE INSTITUTE OF RELIGION

Continuing aboveground across Wilkins Street, you will reach the Texas Medical Center Park, a lovely area of rustic shelter and outdoor tranquility, located in the Institute of Religion Plaza (between Methodist Hospital and Texas Woman's University).

The Institute of Religion was chartered in 1955 as an interfaith center for graduate and continuing education and research in pastoral ministry, religion and health, and ethics in medicine.

LAURENCE FAVROT HALL

This is a residence hall administered by Texas Medical Center.

TEXAS WOMAN'S UNIVERSITY— HOUSTON CENTER

TWU is the largest women's university in the United States. Its main campus is located in Denton. The Houston Center, opened in 1960, offers nursing and allied health educational courses to

men and women. There are two instructional buildings and two residence halls in this complex.

UT DENTAL BRANCH

The Dental Branch, part of the University of Texas Health Science Center at Houston, is across Bertner Avenue from the Institute of Religion, across Moursund Avenue from Baylor College of Medicine, and across a parking lot from M. D. Anderson Hospital and Tumor Institute.

The school has a clinic where dental students, dental hygienists, and dental assistants receive much of their training.

JESSE H. JONES LIBRARY BUILDING

Walk past the Alkek Fountain at Baylor College of Medicine. On M. D. Anderson Boulevard, visit the Medical Center's library building, which contains the Houston Academy of Medicine—Texas Medical Center Library. This library is shared by the institutions of the Medical Center and includes a special Patient Information Collection (ask the librarian to show the way).

Also housed in the Jones Library Building are Texas Medical Center (the planning and coordinating body for the center), the Harris County Medical Society, and the Doctors' Club (a private restaurant and social club).

UT MEDICAL SCHOOL AND UT SCHOOL OF ALLIED HEALTH SCIENCES

Adjacent to the Jesse H. Jones Library Building are the John H. Freeman Building and the UT Medical School Building. Both are components of the University of Texas Health Science Center at Houston. (UTHSCH also includes the Dental Branch, Graduate School of Biomedical Sciences, School of Public Health, School of Nursing, Division of Continuing Education, Speech and Hearing Institute, and Mental Sciences Institute.)

The School of Allied Health Sciences offers training in many undergraduate and graduate allied health programs, and the UT Medical School is known for its outstanding education and research.

Hermann Hospital is the primary teaching hospital for UTHSCH. Training is also provided at M. D. Anderson, Texas Heart Institute, and St. Luke's Episcopal Hospital, as well as other hospitals in the Medical Center, the city, and the state.

UTHSCH's cafeteria is located on the Hermann Hospital side of Ross Sterling Avenue.

The peaceful C. Frank Webber Plaza separates the Medical School and the library building. Two sculptures in the plaza are gifts of Dr. Richard S. Ruiz. *Woman with Dove* above the fountain, by Prince Monyo Mihailescu-Nasturel of Rumania, is in honor of his mother. The untitled work by Hous-

HERMANN PARK

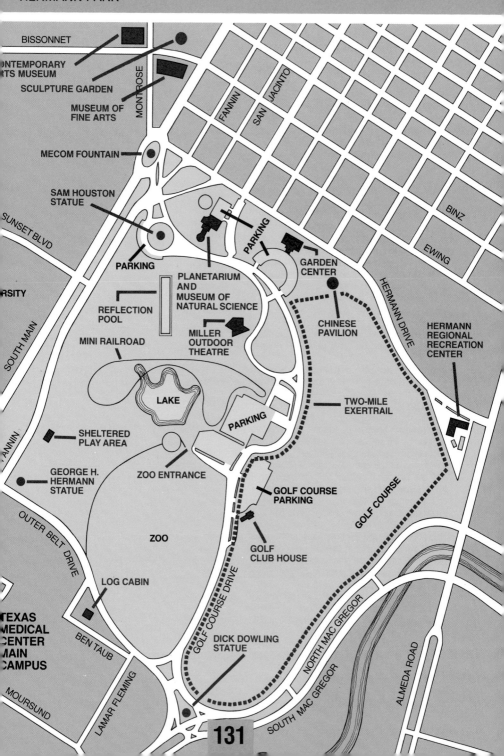

BISSONNET

CONTEMPORARY
ARTS MUSEUM

SCULPTURE GARDEN

MUSEUM OF
FINE ARTS

MONTROSE

FANNIN

SAN JACINTO

BINZ

EWING

MECOM FOUNTAIN

SAM HOUSTON
STATUE

SUNSET BLVD

PARKING

PARKING

GARDEN
CENTER

RSITY

REFLECTION
POOL

PLANETARIUM
AND
MUSEUM OF
NATURAL SCIENCE

CHINESE
PAVILION

HERMANN DRIVE

HERMANN
REGIONAL
RECREATION
CENTER

SOUTH MAIN

MINI RAILROAD

MILLER
OUTDOOR
THEATRE

LAKE

TWO-MILE
EXERTRAIL

ANNIN

SHELTERED
PLAY AREA

PARKING

GEORGE H.
HERMANN
STATUE

ZOO ENTRANCE

GOLF COURSE
PARKING

GOLF COURSE

ZOO

GOLF
CLUB HOUSE

OUTER BELT DRIVE

LOG CABIN

GOLF COURSE DRIVE

NORTH MAC GREGOR

ALMEDA ROAD

TEXAS
MEDICAL
CENTER
MAIN
CAMPUS

BEN TAUB

DICK DOWLING
STATUE

LAMAR FLEMING

MOURSUND

SOUTH MAC GREGOR

ton sculptor Robert Fowler, a twelve-foot-tall construction of corten steel, which quickly oxidizes to
produce a rusty color, honors his father. Webber
Plaza is occasionally the site of concerts at noon.

HERMANN PARK

Take your picnic lunch to the park. There are
tables scattered about and many things to do, look
at, or watch.

Hermann Park, across Outer Belt Drive from the
Medical Center, covers 545 acres and is bounded
by Fannin Street, Almeda Road, and Hermann
Drive. It has children's playgrounds, picnic facilities, ballfields, a recreation center, a jogger's exertrail, an eighteen-hole golf course and clubhouse,
a zoo (with a separate children's zoo), an aquar-
ium, a passenger-carrying miniature train, a garden center (with a special section for the blind,
which has plants to be identified by smell and
Braille signs), a pagoda, an outdoor theater on a
grassy hill, museums of natural and medical sciences, a planetarium, statues, sculptures, fountains, ponds, and a lake (where those under 12
and over 65 are permitted to fish). Most of it
is free.

Walk through the park just to look at the sculptures, statues, and fountains: *George H. Hermann*
by Lonnie Edwards at Outer Belt Drive and Fannin
Street across from Hermann Hospital; *Atropos Key,*
a bronze sculpture by Hannah Stewart near Miller
Outdoor Theatre; *Simón Bolívar* donated by the
consul general of Venezuela, *Kasuga Stone Lantern*
donated by Chiba City, Japan, and *José de San
Martín* (with a pedestal by Tommy Schlitzberger)
donated by the Argentine community of Houston
in the International Sculpture Garden; *The Group*
by Charles Umlauf at the Museum of Natural History; the wonderful *Untitled* welded-steel elephant
by Bob Fowler at the entrance to the zoo; the
bronze monument *General Sam Houston,* the first
president of the Republic of Texas, who points
to the San Jacinto Battlegrounds where he won
Texas' independence from Mexico with the defeat
of Santa Anna, located at the northwest corner of
Hermann Park; and the granite statue *Dick Dowling,* a Civil War hero, at North MacGregor Drive
and Hermann Loop Drive.

Fountains in the park include Bird Fountain, Fra-
grant Garden Fountain, Mecom-Rockwell Fountain,
Rain Forest Waterfall, Lilian Schnitzer Memorial
Fountain, and, at the zoo, Brownie Fountain and
Rain Forest Waterfall. At the intersection of Fan-
nin, Main, and Montrose streets is the landmark
Mecom Fountain.

There are, of course, many sculptures and
works of art at the nearby Museum of Fine Arts
and the Contemporary Arts Museum.

DIAGNOSTIC CLINIC OF HOUSTON

6448 Fannin St. (77030)
713/797-9191
Security: 790-0790

HOURS
M–F, 8:30 AM–5 PM
Emergency: 24 hours daily
PARKING
Diagnostic Center Hospital garage; valet
parking at Clinic entrance for disabled
RECEPTION
Lobby

PARKING   TUNNELS   SKYWALKS   METRO ROUTES: A   B   C

In 1957, a group of nine physicians joined forces to develop a group practice in which their services, along with those of nurses, technical personnel, and administrative staff, were combined to deliver quality health care.

In 1958, the new organization completed and occupied a two-story facility, located on Fannin Street across from the Texas Medical Center.

By 1966, the pressing demand for additional patient beds in the Medical Center area caused the clinic physicians to encourage construction of a 150-bed hospital adjacent to their building. Another major development program was started in 1969. The hospital doubled in size to its present 300 beds, and a new eight-story office tower was erected. Seven floors of space were added in 1977; and in 1982, the Diagnostic Clinic celebrated its twenty-fifth anniversary by occupying thirteen thousand additional square feet in the new facility.

This ambulatory outpatient clinic is unique because its services are largely confined to the field of internal medicine. All medical subspecialties are included in order to offer comprehensive capability and support for the mission of the clinic. Medical evaluation and treatment are available in the following fields: cardiology, endocrinology, geriatrics, hematology, gastroenterology, infectious diseases, neurology, oncology, pulmonary diseases, nephrology, and rheumatology. Additional subspecialties related to internal medicine, including radiology, pathology, nuclear medicine, dermatology, and allergy, are also provided.

The clinic has no surgical specialties as part of the group practice; however, surgical consultants in all fields are readily available for surgical evaluation and treatment.

The Diagnostic Clinic deals with over 100,000 patients per year, making it one of the largest clinics in the United States. The original staff has grown from nine to sixty-eight physicians. Over 17,000 new patients come annually for services ranging from periodic health examinations to evaluation and treatment of complex diseases.

This proprietary organization offers a private practice environment in which each patient is assured the right to informed choice and privacy. Patients are either self-referred or physician referred. In addition to diagnostic services and medical evaluation, treatment and follow-up are a part of the normal routine.

Patients, who come from all parts of the United States, Mexico, and South America, find many advanced capabilities in the Diagnostic Clinic. These include computerized tomography, nuclear imaging, ultrasound, nerve conduction studies, Doppler evaluations, radioimmunoassay procedures, stress testing, hemodialysis, chemotherapy,

laser skin surgery, evoked response techniques, electromyography, subtraction angiography, and transluminal balloon angioplasty.

A special translation service is available for Spanish to English. Several individual physicians are fluent in other languages.

FOOD SERVICE
A cafeteria, open daily (6:30 AM to 6:30 PM) for breakfast, lunch, and dinner, is located on the first floor of the Diagnostic Center Hospital.

SHOPPING FACILITIES
A gift shop is located on the first floor of the Diagnostic Center Hospital. It offers a variety of cards, candies, magazines, newspapers, books, stamps, flowers, and gift items. It is open Monday through Friday, 9:00 AM to 1:30 PM and 2:00 PM to 5:00 PM.

GENERAL INFORMATION
The Diagnostic Clinic employs a social worker, who can be reached through the main clinic telephone number. Wheelchairs are provided for those who are disabled or cannot walk. Patient assistance is on hand in the clinic lobby.

KELSEY-SEYBOLD CLINIC, P.A.

6624 Fannin St. (77030)
713/797-1551

HOURS
Clinic: M–F, 8 AM–5:30 PM
Emergency: 24 hours daily
PARKING
Clinic parking bldg.
RECEPTION
Ground floor lobby

PARKING   TUNNELS   SKYWALKS   METRO ROUTES: A   B   C

The Kelsey-Seybold Clinic began in 1949 as the private practice of Texan Mavis P. Kelsey, M.D. The practice expanded and was known as the Kelsey and Leary Clinic (after William V. Leary, M.D.). When it moved to its present location at the Texas Medical Center in 1963, it was called the Kelsey-Leary-Seybold Clinic (with the addition of William D. Seybold, M.D.). Dr. Leary retired in 1965, and the name was changed to Kelsey-Seybold.

Today there are ten additional clinics providing most specialty and subspecialty services for people in Houston and surrounding communities. Over six hundred patients are seen each day in Kelsey-Seybold's Medical Center clinic, more than a thousand in the various outlying offices; nearly a million patients have been treated since this complex opened. It has become the largest group practice in the greater Houston area.

Although Kelsey-Seybold is oriented to private consultation, it has become an extension of the Medical Center. It is a for-profit, outpatient, multi-specialty facility, providing health care to individuals, families, corporations, and government centers. When necessary, patients are hospitalized at nearby St. Luke's Episcopal Hospital, Texas Children's Hospital, or Methodist Hospital. The clinic admits patients without referrals, and patients may choose their doctors.

The clinic is affiliated with Baylor College of Medicine in a teaching program for medical students, interns, and residents. Students from other universities also rotate through the clinic's specialty departments.

The nonprofit Kelsey-Seybold Foundation, organized in 1956, makes a notable contribution by providing financial support for research through fellowships and grants for specific projects in clinical investigation and basic research. Work on cancer at the Crump Center for Clinical Cancer Research and the Vercellino Center for Gastrointestinal Cancer Research are two such efforts. Current studies are centered on cancer prevention, its early diagnosis, and its treatment. Other research is focused on preventive medicine in heart disease and diabetes. Also through the support of the foundation, the clinic is developing an ambulatory treatment center for diabetes.

Kelsey-Seybold also has an affiliation with M. D. Anderson Hospital and Tumor Institute. Joint cancer research projects include the Crump Fellowship for Clinical Cancer, a study on the early detection of cancer in the general patient population, and a study of tumor markers. The two institutions cooperate in a patient referral program and in mutual staff appointments. Most of

this work is done through the Kelsey-Seybold Foundation.

Kelsey-Seybold's broad purpose is complete medical care. It is a health care facility for the whole family, from pediatrics to geriatrics, where the patient-physician relationship is paramount. Patients are accepted directly or are referred to one of the many specialty departments. The clinic has a referral practice from the United States, Latin America, Europe, and the Middle East, drawing people from all around the world.

The clinic has special equipment and facilities in dietetics, audiology, electroencephalography, electromyography, and electronystagmography. Kelsey-Seybold has a pulmonary function laboratory and complete facilities in nuclear medicine, radiology, and endoscopy. The clinic has a Linares imaging center, which provides whole-body scanning and ultrasound examinations. There is a clinic specializing in aviation medicine, where pilots are examined for FAA medical certificates. Certain departments handle interpreting skills and patient education. Kelsey-Seybold supports a regional immunization center and provides physical therapy, speech therapy, and classes in weight reduction, smoking cessation, stress management, nutrition, physical fitness, and cardiac rehabilitation.

Kelsey-Seybold offers specialized health care and extensive occupational medicine programs for many industries and the U.S. government. Environmental health services include industrial hygiene, health physics, and environmental laboratory analysis. Experts search for potential health hazards; devise solutions to meet OSHA, NIOSH, and EPA regulations; and teach employees how to protect themselves. The clinic conducts employee screening programs, health education series, and physical fitness classes and provides specialty physician or nursing services.

Kelsey-Seybold is under government contract for on-site medical services at five NASA locations. Offices are at the Johnson Space Center in Houston; Langley Research Center in Hampton, Virginia; and Marshall Space Flight Center in Huntsville, Alabama. Physicians and technicians have contributed to the Apollo, Skylab, Apollo-Soyuz, and Shuttle programs. They have worked on health stabilization projects, carried out critical mission examinations, given medical support in mission control, and served as examining doctors for astronauts.

Kelsey-Seybold maintains a contact with the Great Lakes Naval Regional Medical Center in Illinois. Medical personnel have also worked with the Department of Defense in an Air Force health study. Specialty services are provided for the National Maritime Union in Houston.

Kelsey-Seybold's goal is and will continue to be providing cost-effective preventive medicine and total health care. Its Medical Center clinic will become more important as a tertiary care center for referrals from Kelsey-Seybold satellite offices and from outside sources.

FOOD SERVICE
For patients and visitors, there is only limited food service from vending machines. A daily luncheon is provided for doctors, visiting physicians, residents, and medical students. Since this is a time when doctors meet, the luncheons are not open to the public.

GUIDED TOURS
Tours are specially arranged for visiting physicians and other medical personnel.

VOLUNTEERS
The Kelsey-Seybold Foundation is setting up a volunteer program for the cancer research centers. More information can be obtained by calling 797-0507.

GENERAL INFORMATION
The clinic has an interpreting department for the many patients from other countries who do not speak English. Interpreters are available for Arabic, Chinese, French, German, Hebrew, Italian, Persian, and Spanish. Patients who are coming from out of town may call the department of Patient Relations for assistance with hotel arrangements.

A pharmacy is located near the clinic entrance in the parking garage building. It is open from 8:00 AM to 5:30 PM, Monday through Friday.

Kelsey-Seybold presents various educational and self-improvement programs. Instructional films cover such subjects as pregnancy and diabetes. Classes are taught in weight loss, smoking cessation, stress management, physical fitness, cardiac rehabilitation, and nutrition.

Kelsey-Seybold Clinic has joined with Maxicare Texas, Inc., a health maintenance organization, to offer a prepaid health care insurance plan to employees (and their families) of business and industries. Maxicare stresses preventive care in addition to treating illnesses and injuries. Patients choose their personal physician at any Kelsey-Seybold clinic, make appointments as they wish, and receive medical treatment without annual deductibles and claim forms. Hospital, home care, and related treatments are offered at no, or low, charge.

CHECK-IN/CHECK-OUT
New patients are issued a clinic identification card on their first visit. It is helpful thereafter to have the card with its identification number available when calling for an appointment.

Out-of-town patients need to allow three to seven days if they require a comprehensive physical exam.

First-time patients should bring insurance information, Social Security number, and Medicare card.

EMERGENCY ROOM SUGGESTIONS

1. Notify your physician before leaving for the hospital. Treatment can sometimes be hastened if the physician tells emergency room staff of an anticipated arrival. It is possible he or she can meet you there or give the name of a specialist for your particular emergency. Take the name and phone number of your doctor. Hospital personnel can contact him or her for information.

2. Carry with you any medications you take. Treatment can be considerably slowed if you can only offer, "I take three heart medicines." Emergency room personnel need prescription names and dosages. Medical history, including existing or previous illnesses, and allergies, is extremely helpful in an emergency.

3. Take a knowledgeable, supportive person. Usually one person is permitted to remain with the patient.

4. Take any hospital identification card you might have.

5. Take your health insurance card. Complete information, such as Social Security number, and next of kin, is useful.

6. While emergency rooms will not refuse emergency treatment to a child in a life-threatening circumstance, they make every effort to locate parents beforehand. It is helpful to leave a note with a baby sitter or friend if you will be unavailable. A slip giving permission to authorize medical treatment is all that is needed.

7. Do not take valuables.

Most emergency rooms will take major credit cards and checks in addition to cash for payment. Some will even bill a patient or insurance company. Most people do not know the particulars of their insurance coverage, especially if they are covered in a group policy by their employer. For that reason, some hospitals are reluctant to bill insurance companies.

STREET NAMES

Streets in the Texas Medical Center area were originally designated by numbers and letters. Avenues ran north-south and streets ran east-west. The names were changed to permanently honor the benefactors of the Medical Center, beginning with M. D. Anderson Boulevard in 1949.

M. D. Anderson Boulevard
Monroe D. Anderson, originally a banker from Tennessee, was the financial advisor for Anderson, Clayton & Company, a cotton merchandising concern founded by his brother and a partner. Mr. Anderson came to Houston in 1907 at the age of 34. He never married. In 1936, he created the M. D. Anderson Foundation with himself and his friends Colonel William B. Bates and John Freeman as trustees. The foundation, then worth $300,000, received over $19 million from his estate when he died in 1939.

Bates Street
Colonel William B. Bates was a friend and fishing companion of Monroe D. Anderson. Mr. Anderson chose him (along with John Freeman) as a trustee of the M. D. Anderson Foundation. "Colonel" was an honorary title bestowed upon him by his friend Governor Dan Moody, and he was called that from affection and respect. Colonel Bates was a partner in the law firm Fulbright, Crooker, Freeman and Bates, which handled legal business for Anderson, Clayton & Company. Mr. Bates died in 1974 at the age of 85.

Bellows Lane
Warren S. Bellows, best known for the work of his construction firm, built many of the landmark buildings in Houston, in addition to the San Jacinto Monument, erected to commemorate the victory of Texas over Mexico in the battle on that site. He was named as a trustee of the M. D. Anderson Foundation in 1954, filling the vacancy created by the death of Horace Wilkins. Mr. Bellows headed a successful campaign to raise over a million dollars for the University of Texas units, the cancer research center, and the dental school. He was an active leader in many civic, artistic, cultural, and educational efforts in Harris County.

Bertner Avenue
Dr. E. William Bertner was a prominent Houston physician who helped bring a cancer research hospital to Houston. He lived at the Rice Hotel on the same floor as his friend John Freeman. He was the acting director of M. D. Anderson Hospital during its first years, was the first president of the Texas Medical Center, and died of cancer in 1950.

East Cullen Street
Hugh Roy Cullen was one of the first trustees of the newly formed Texas Medical Center. He entered the oil business when he came to Houston in 1911 and became one of the most successful wildcatters in Texas. In 1947, he and his wife, Lillie,

established the Cullen Foundation, endowed with thousands of acres of oil lands. Mr. Cullen died in 1957, but his foundation continues to benefit the Medical Center.

Lamar Fleming Street
Lamar Fleming was chairman of the board of Anderson, Clayton & Company. He and his wife made many contributions to the Medical Center, including the endowment of a fund at Baylor College of Medicine and the donation of an annex at M. D. Anderson Hospital and Tumor Institute.

John Freeman Avenue
John Henry Freeman was a partner in Fulbright, Crooker, Freeman and Bates, the law firm for Anderson, Clayton & Company. Monroe D. Anderson named him (along with Colonel Bates) as an original trustee of the M. D. Anderson Foundation, a position he held until his death in 1980.

Richard J. V. Johnson Avenue
Richard J. V. Johnson, currently serving as president of the *Houston Chronicle,* one of America's leading newspapers, was previously chairman of the board of the Medical Center. Well known for his many civic activities, Johnson continued the tradition that links the center with the mainstream of Houston activity.

Moursund Avenue
Walter Henrik Moursund was the first dean of Baylor University College of Medicine (now Baylor College of Medicine). He died in 1959.

Herman Pressler Boulevard
Herman Pressler, an attorney, was a director and vice-president of Humble Oil & Refining Company (now Exxon Company USA). Born in 1902, he has devoted years of his life to community service through contributions to both the Texas Medical Center and several of its institutions. A founder and member of the board of Texas Children's Hospital since its beginning in 1950, he chaired that board from 1976 to 1982, when he became chairman emeritus. He has been on the Board of Directors of the Texas Medical Center since 1972 and was its president from 1976 to 1981. Additionally, he served as chairman of the Joint Operating Committee of St. Luke's Episcopal and Texas Children's hospitals and Texas Heart Institute from its creation in 1970 until 1980. Mr. Pressler has also served as a trustee of Baylor College of Medicine since 1976.

Ross Sterling Avenue
Ross Sterling was an oilman-publisher. He organized Humble Oil Company (now Exxon Company USA) in 1917 and combined two newspapers to create the *Houston Post.* Mr. Sterling, who established Houston's first commercial radio station, was governor of Texas from 1931 to 1933. He served on the Hermann Hospital Estate Board and was elected its president in 1946. He remained a member of the board until his death in 1949.

Wilkins Street
Horace M. Wilkins was president of the State National Bank of Houston (now First City National Bank). In 1940, after the death of Monroe D. Anderson, he was named successor trustee to the M. D. Anderson Foundation by Colonel William B. Bates and John Freeman. Mr. Wilkins was one of the early supporters of the Texas Medical Center and was active in the civic, charitable, and religious affairs of Houston. He died in 1953.

TEXAS A&M UNIVERSITY INSTITUTE OF BIOSCIENCES AND TECHNOLOGY
Four major research programs are underway at the Texas A&M University Institute of Biosciences and Technology, which has become the thirty-eighth organization in Texas Medical Center. A twenty-two-story building is planned to house these advanced efforts and will be under construction during 1988.

INDEX

Vercellino Center for Gastrointestinal Cancer
    Research, 137
Veterans Administration Medical Center, 5,
    11, 38, 56, 79, 108–110, 117, 127
Visitor Information Center, 7, 8–9

walking tour, 127–132
Wilkins, Horace M., 2, 139, 140
Williams, Wheeler, 82